Keep Showing Up

A Memoir and Powerful Guidebook for Empaths to Embody Self-Love, Self-Empowerment, and Self-Worth

Kara Karaoguz

For permissions contact: hello@karakaraoguz.com

Cover photo by Amanda Kinton Photography

ISBN: 978-1-7353060-0-1

Facebook: Kara Karaoguz

Private FB Group: Intuitive Self Healers

IG: @kara_karaoguz

Dedicated to the Empaths and Truth Seekers
showing up to Do The Work.
Deep peace is available to you.
You can break the cycle.

I'm here for it.

XO

KEEP SHOWING UP

CONTENTS

Keep Showing Up

PREFACE

This book has found its way into your hands for a purpose greater than we know. It's meant to wake you up, shake you up, and lovingly light a fire under your ass to inspire you to make the changes in your life you know you need to make.

I know this about you: You are a strong, ambitious, empathic, intuitive, loving, compassionate woman with a history of trauma and sketchy boundaries. What are boundaries, anyways?! Blurred lines. You. Love. Hard. You know you're a good person, easy to get along with yet you find yourself in dysfunctional relationship dynamics. That's not working for you anymore. You're ready for a new reality.

You're sick of doubting yourself, not believing in yourself, of spreading yourself too thin for the sake of others. You're tired of seeking external validation and looking for approval from others who can barely give it to themselves. You are so over feeling super sensitive to others, having low self esteem, sabotaging yourself and not trusting others. Ugh.

You're ready to step into your highest potential, the Next Level version of yourself. You're ready to identify your power, love yourself in ways you never thought possible, experience trust and respect for yourself that you've never known before. Here now, you're ready to co-create the life of your dreams through manifestation, utilizing the Law Of Attraction (LOA). You're ready to feel empowered by honoring and trusting your own intuition and build confidence as a strong adult female, healing the wounds of your inner child. You're ready to end the relationships that are toxic or dragging you down. You're ready to live your best life!!

Keep Showing Up is a memoir, peppered with spirituality and guidance, psychological perspectives, physiological realities and powerful lessons to give you tools to embody massive amounts of self confidence. You are gonna master the shit out of self love! You will naturally create healthy boundaries as an expression of self assurance signifying the strong woman you are growing into. You'll learn about self-empowerment and radical acceptance for daysssss! Through reading this book, you'll learn to never settle again and you'll truly embody your worth. At any age!!

When I think of this title phrase: "Keep Showing Up", it means despite all the "struggles" or hard times we may have, the ability to continually be here, now, doing your best with the level of understanding, awareness and knowledge you have. Each day will inevitably look different for you as you just Keep Showing Up!!

This book is the story of my destruction, more than once in this lifetime and my subsequent rebirth, recreation and rebuilding of an amazing life I co-create every single day.

Part I is My Story. Part II is The Lessons, a chance for you to Do The Work. You can complete the reflective entries and journaling prompts here in the book or your own journal. It's up to you. Part III is the Wrap Up, bringing all the pieces together.

Though I have left space in the book for answering the prompts and reflective questions in Part II, I recommend having a separate journal in case you want to write more than the space allows for.

Journaling has been incredibly therapeutic for me in my healing. Your journal provides a sacred space to unpack and hold your wounds, while you uncover deeply buried memories, excavating the landscape of your inner world, processing and integrating safely.

Remember, Keep Showing Up. This is your journey, this is your life, these are your practices to incorporate into changing your lifestyle. If you get to a point where it feels like too much emotion, if you're feeling overwhelmed then allow yourself to take a break and do something nurturing. Love on yourself.

I invite your correspondence anytime via email:
hello@karakaraoguz.com

I work privately with clients in a 1:1 capacity as well as in Online Group Coaching programs. If you're ready to do the work and open to me as your guide, let's do it! Book a free Exploration Call to be sure we're a good fit. www.karakaraoguz.com For now, enjoy this phenomenal resource I created for you!

If you are an Empath (which you likely are if you are reading this), please take the necessary shielding measures as you read through the first part of this book. If you are unaware go any, you will learn some. **Trigger warning**, fo sho. And possibly cleanse your space with sage after. Just looking out for you babes. My hope is that this book will become part of your survival-to-thrival guide.

Empaths CHECKLIST

@kara_karaoguz

✓ You feel the emotions of others and tend to absorb them

✓ You are easily drained by anyone negative or pessimistic, actually repulsed by the toxicity

✓ You are Highly Sensitive and get overwhelmed in large crowds

✓ You are unable to watch violence, tragedy, horror, the news

✓ You need quiet, alone time to recharge preferably in nature

✓ You KNOW when others are lying, being dishonest or two faced, easily sensing a shift in energetic vibration

✓ You are a natural healer, drawn to helping others

✓ Strangers or Acquaintances confide in you or look to you for advice

✓ You are highly intuitive

www.karakaraoguz.com

This is a checklist of SOME of the qualities that Empaths embody. Do you see yourself on this list?

PART I

I tell my story so others know they can heal too.

Chapter 1

"Oh It Happened"

"Trauma is a fact of life. It does not, however, have to be a life sentence." -Peter Levine

I looked out over the microphone that had been angled to an appropriate height for my small body to see a nearly empty courtroom. I cried and shuddered, placing both hands over my face in an attempt to hide, shoulders hunched forward. To my left sat twelve jurors, all wide eyed, staring at me with a softness I remember seeing through the tears of my blurred vision. To my right sat the judge, a tall authoritative man. In front of me I saw my aunt whose attempts to give me reassuring gestures did not go unnoticed. I remember seeing my legal representation, a round woman with the sweetest demeanor. Then looking to the right of them sat "the accused": my mother's ex-boyfriend, with his legal representation. He hired a prominent defense attorney, which to me even at a young age, meant he knew he needed all the help he could get to dismiss the charges.

I was twelve years old. I was about to endure a week of testifying against my abuser for sexually molesting me. I felt intense embarrassment, shame, a desire to not be seen, to not have all those eyes on me.

I remember I had practiced walking into the vacant courtroom before the trial, doing a "dry run" of entering the doors, walking behind the bleacher-esque seats the jurors sat in then all the way to the witness stand. Despite that, nothing could have prepared me for this.

I don't remember much about that week, other than answering questions about what I experienced over a four year period when my innocence was taken. It was during that time my view of love got completely twisted.

At one point I remember the defense attorney asking me about my favorite movies and music I listened to. I loved Dirty Dancing for the love story (and still do!) and of course: Madonna. It was the 1980's. Her music was extremely influential for our whole culture. These were his attempts to paint me as a liar, a sexually charged child placing false blame on an innocent until proven guilty adult. It disgusts me to think back on that rationale, as my adult self; how could this person sleep at night??

After a week of testimonies, that mutherfucker was found not guilty on all charges.

The only charge I remember was "endangering the welfare of a child". Hearing the juror representative repeatedly say "Not Guilty" to all the charges made my head spin and heart sink.

Apparently for the aforementioned charge to count in New York, the abuse needed to have gone on for a minimum of two years. Two years?! Two- effing years.

When I had initially told my mom about the abuse, within weeks I had to sit in front of a Grand Jury. Those jurors deemed my story as truthful and worthy of charges. At that time, before months of therapy, I had a recollection of it all going on for a year and a half, so apparently that's what I said when I first testified in Grand Jury before it all went to trial. In the time between Grand Jury and the trial, I was talking with a counselor weekly and uncovered the four years of abuse, from age six to ten. I remember being in fifth grade, watching a VHS tape about inappropriate touches and the importance of telling someone you trust. I was sitting in the back row (still my style), looking around at my peers realizing what I had been experiencing wasn't "normal". It was earth shattering.

According to my legal representation in her explanation to me after the verdict was read, they went on the transcripts from Grand Jury. She did her best to quell my confusion. It still didn't make sense to me. What I said in my testimony for the trial didn't matter. After all that, he walked. Karma caught up with him eventually when he fell off a ladder on my birthday, thirteen years later. The fall resulted in a traumatic brain injury, leaving him captive in his own useless body.

* * *

As a young adult, I went to the local courthouse to get the transcripts of my trial. As part of my healing journey then I was curious exactly what they asked me, who else testified, what was said, etc.

When I inquired, the clerk couldn't find any record of them.

I persisted and he asked: "Well, what was the verdict?"

I said "He was acquitted."

"Oh I won't find them then."

Perplexed and getting defensive, I challenged him: "Why? What does that mean?"

He replied, very nonchalantly: "It means it never happened."

I was so pissed, I could feel my heart race, my face get hot and a lump gathering in my throat.

"Oh, it happened." I said, looking him in the eyes and turning to walk out the door.

Since then, I haven't done any other digging to get access to the transcripts from June of 1992. That whole exchange was quite discouraging and embarrassment flooded my system again, as another person tried to take away my truth.

* * *

By the following summer, my adolescent rebellious reign began. I was out many nights, walking the city streets of my hometown with my best friend. One night, we found ourselves hanging with a boy I liked. Somehow I ended up with this person in our friend's father's bed (so gross just thinking about it). I was thirteen, about to have sex for the first time against my will.

I said "no, wait, I don't want to," with his heavy body on top of me.

He said "just for a minute" while forcing his way inside me.

My body was frozen. I cried, a silent hot tear streamed down the right side of my face. It hurt. I felt so disgusted. Then it was over.

It took me years to understand that this was rape. I didn't fight him off but I still said "No". I now understand that my body went into the dorsal vagal activation. My autonomic nervous system took over to keep me protected, much like the limp state an animal goes into if it's being eaten. You'll learn more on that in Part II.

In the short period of time between those two recollections is another instance of extreme betrayal by a close family member. This one affected me the most. The violations occurred over the course of a couple months. My trust was shattered by someone who wasn't supposed to hurt me, yet again. It is really challenging to recover from things like this. I see now that healing is an ongoing process. It's like a spiral. We loop back around again and again until that which once hurt so bad has no feeling associated with it. It's a lifestyle to Keep Showing Up.

* * *

Through my adolescence, the last thing I wanted was to feel rejected. To feel not accepted by the guys I "hung out" with would have been crushing. So as a result, I betrayed myself and my own needs, putting them first so they would like me. I spent most of my days stoned. I smoked weed on my way to school with friends, leaving throughout the day to get a coffee and get high again, then typically leaving school early to go smoke, hang out, listen to music, hike. I was also smoking cigarettes from thirteen on. I barely passed High School, graduating with the bare minimum requirements. I was just going through the motions, living on autopilot, completely disconnected from my power.

I continued my education at the local community college. Little did I know I was on the verge of a tremendous shift in my life.

KEEP SHOWING UP

CHAPTER 2

Greater Awareness

"When we have the courage to walk into our story and own it, we get to write the ending." -Brene Brown

I lay on the gym mats at the community college, cocooned in my comforter during savasana, the corpse pose, after a two hour yoga practice. I was nineteen. I chose yoga to get PE credits towards my first degree. The instructor was certified from Kripalu, a wellness retreat center in the Berkshire mountains of Massachusetts.

Leaving class every Monday night for a whole semester, I remember feeling like I was floating on air. So euphoric and at peace. This was a feeling I had never felt before. The instructor opened my eyes, ears, heart, soul to the ability to access this peace anytime I wanted. And I wanted it. She gave me the awareness that yoga is more than the poses we do on the mats and in class, it's a way of life.

The following semester, I chose another elective course called Therapeutic Touch, which supported this entry into the world of energy healing. I was very curious about this bold new world that really wasn't talked about much, especially in my western medicine based family.

Years later, with a Bachelor of Arts in Psychology under my belt, I was bound and determined to help survivors heal from abuse. I was still committed to my yoga practice and also began dabbling in Reiki, Cranio-Sacral Therapy (CST), massage therapy, women's healing circles, crystals, essential oils, and the like. A lover of our solar system, I began following the moon cycles and tuning into astrology. In my studies of yoga, I learned all about our subtle body and the chakra system as part of my own healing and growth.

To continue my studies of energy healing, I got certified in the Bach Flower Essences and attuned as a Reiki II practitioner. Working with the energy fields was and still is fascinating to me. We have the power to heal ourselves, it's just a matter of learning to seek out the appropriate supports, guiding us in the right direction. #selfhealers

At this point in my love life, I had been coupled with the same man for many years. He was very supportive of all my spiritual endeavors and encouraged my growth. However, when we had conflict, we had conflict. Neither of us knew how to effectively navigate or repair so a lot of damage was inflicted. I know now, we were energetically matched up to show one another our deep core wounds so we could heal them ourselves. A major issue was our outlook on intimate relations. If he initiated sex and I wasn't feeling it, he would take that as rejection and show up as a lower frequency version of himself, often breaking things and yelling. In Part II, you will read about emotional states and their corresponding energetic frequency. His actions threw me further into a withdrawn state with my walls up and no desire for connection. At times, because of the arguing it didn't feel safe. For a trauma survivor, feeling SAFE is of the utmost importance. Once that safety is gone, much like trust, it's a challenge to get back.

* * *

We purposefully conceived a child in love and welcomed a baby boy into the world in 2005. He was perfect though my birth experience was not. The culture of birth in this country is so messed up, with so many women experiencing traumatic births. When I think back on my first birth, it's oddly familiar. I didn't realize at the time that I felt completely victimized all over again by my OB/GYN, someone I trusted. Much like my abuser in my childhood.

I was induced when I was 40 weeks and 3 days. In hindsight, I could have declined the option of induction. Because I went along with that, I missed a surprise party for my maternal grandmother's 80th birthday! Not only was I disappointed about that, I had every intervention that come before a cesarean. I don't talk about it much because one of the main tenants of HypnoBirthing is for expectant moms to only saturate their minds with positive birth stories. I don't ever want to add to anyone's fear or anxiety by sharing what I went through.

* * *

I was fortunate to be able to stay home with my new baby and cultivate a very trusting stable relationship with him. Having my degree in Psychology with many of my electives taken related to child development, I understood the importance of giving my babes a strong foundation for his first three years. We had so much fun during this time. I always look back very fondly on these years together.

This was around the time *The Secret* came out and I was enthralled. The Law Of Attraction made perfect sense to me. Understanding the power of words, our thoughts, our languaging, our energy was like coming home. I effortlessly incorporated my new learnings into my life.

I read and fell in love with the book *You Can Heal Your Life* by Louise Hay. She too had a history of childhood sexual abuse so I felt connected to her in that sense. Her teachings involved using the power of the mind, incorporating positive affirmations into our lives so as to bring great healing. That all resonated with me too, as an eternal optimist. I always look for the good in people and it seemed she did too.

There was another TV series I would watch called "Starting Over" about a group of women who moved into a house where two life coaches (Iyanla Vanzant and Rhonda Britten) would give them personal development assignments and work through healing practices together. I used to take notes on things they would talk about or activities they would do to heal. This has always felt right to me. Always part of my path.

* * *

Just before getting pregnant with our second son, I had been taking a
new birth control pill for about six weeks when I noticed I had all the
adverse effects just shy of blood clots leading to DVT or Stroke. The
most debilitating was the panic attacks that would come out of
nowhere. I was typically very calm and grounded so when these acute
states of anxiety flared up I was scared. I approached my OB/GYN to
address my concerns. This was the same one who was
condescending, demeaning and bullied the nurses during my birth; I
should have known better, thinking she would be accepting of my
experience.

Sitting down together in an emergency visit I had scheduled the day
before (per guidance of my counselor at the time), I began to explain
what I was experiencing: unrelenting anxiety, panic attacks, night
sweats, extreme weight loss (15lbs on my already small frame in such
a short time), weakness to the point where I couldn't carry our
laundry hampers up or down the stairs-I had to thump them down
each step and it would almost knock me over, dizziness, fatigue, dry,
itchy, irritated eyes. I had also handed her a piece of paper detailing
my side effects for my medical chart. She had no time or tolerance for
my words.

She interrupted me: "Let me stop you right there," with a slight side
to side nod of her tilted head and her index finger pointed upwards.

She then went on in attempts to disprove how any of what I was experiencing was related to the new birth control pills I had been taking. For me, I know my body and that was the only change I could think of and the timing made sense to me. I had just started taking these synthetic hormones then alllllllll this stuff started up. We went back and forth until, with me advocating for myself questioning how she prescribes these meds to her patients. The reason being: I had originally requested this specific birth control per recommendations of a friend because it had the same level of hormone the whole month, with hopes I would feel more stable. She was agreeable at that time (6 weeks prior) and now here I was, in this predicament.

She didn't want to accept any of the responsibility for having prescribed this med and refused to acknowledge the correlation between what I was experiencing and the adverse reactions listed in the medications insert. She didn't want any liability. I wasn't looking for her to "take the blame," I just wanted to be heard and reassured that I wasn't crazy! Eventually she stood up abruptly and said "this isn't going anywhere, I can see you're very set in your beliefs" as she opened the door to usher us out. We walked out of the exam room, me with tears streaming down my face and she stated very loudly: "I won't charge you for today since obviously it didn't help." Cool, thanks.

* * *

I stopped taking the pills and was desperate to get my body back in check. I talked with my uncle one day when all this was going on. He was into natural, "alternative" healing and he suggested acupuncture. I had never tried that and was willing to do anything to feel better.

Excited by this prospect for healing, as soon as we got off the phone, I found a local Licensed Acupuncture/Naturopathic Doctor and called her office. I explained my situation and she graciously squeezed me in for an appointment since it was dire. In talking with her, telling her about my appointment with the OB, she was bewildered that the OB wouldn't have at least considered the possibility that the birth control pills were wreaking havoc in my body.

BTW, these BC pills ended up having huge lawsuits against them for issues similar to mine and worse, though I never pursued a case. I have little faith in the justice system, as you can imagine.

I still remember that first acupuncture treatment, because of my acute state of anxiety it had a tremendous effect on me. She put the needles in, turned on one of my favorite songs, Pachelbel's Canon layered over soothing beach sounds of seagulls and waves crashing, then she quietly closed the door. I'm not sure what happened during that session, though I do know time passed. She was swift and poised as she re-entered the room, gently removed the needles and did some cranio-sacral therapy to further rebalance my system.

Once she was done working her magic, she had me sit up and asked how I was feeling.

Holy shit, I was a new woman!!! I felt a way I had NEVER felt before. Much like the initial feelings after my early days of practicing yoga, it was sheer euphoria. I was floating on a cloud my whole drive home. My body was buzzing. Acupuncture became one of my go-to treatments for rebalancing my chi, my subtle body energy, moving any stagnation and keeping me aligned and well.

* * *

The next month I found out I was pregnant and I would have been damned if I stayed with that same provider. No freaking way. So I left her practice and went in search of another provider to attend the birth of my second baby.

After searching high and low for a holistic practitioner (small town mentality and so many people had no idea what that even meant), I finally came upon a family MD who attended births. When asking if she was holistic (taking the WHOLE person's being into consideration when treating a patient), I was told "if you want a provider who wears Birkenstocks and listens to her patients, she's the one." Sold.

I was so pleased when we had our first visit. She was patient and kind, and very reassuring when it came to easing my mind around being able to have a more empowering experience of birth.

Early on I started attending prenatal yoga classes. I wanted to prepare my body and mind for this birth. I had a traumatic experience with my first son, I was bound to have a more positive experience with my current pregnancy. I treasured my Wednesday night yoga classes because it gave me time to myself. I was still staying home with my son and it was the only time I had away from him.

I really connected with the instructor, the owner of the studio. We clicked right away. We always had heart warming conversations about yoga and life. It was nice being in a class with other expectant moms, going though similar things within their pregnancies.

Eventually towards the end of that pregnancy, I found HypnoBirthing. This is a method of childbirth education based on the premise that birth is a natural, physiological process of the body. The philosophy emphasizes the importance of releasing fear so the birthing muscles and organ can do what it's meant to do. All hypnosis is self-hypnosis; it's basically getting yourself into a deep state of relaxation during labor, along with a slew of other techniques. I dedicated my time to preparing for a calm, peaceful birthing experience, free of any medications or interventions. Going into the birthing experience, my motto was "I'm just gonna see..." I was just gonna see how far I could get without any medications. No pressure, no huge commitment to doing it without drugs to sedate me in some way. Thankfully I was able to pull it off and have an amazing, positive, fun, transformational experience of birth! Yes, laboring and giving birth was fun!! I felt so empowered, knowing what my body was capable of.

I vowed to teach other mothers how to empower themselves through their own experiences of birth. I HAD to share this with anyone who would listen!! Come to find out, many women were craving similar experiences.

CHAPTER 3

Aligned

"Listen to your heart. Because wherever your heart is, that is where you'll find your treasure." -Paolo Coelho

Having decided on my new career path as a Birth Professional, I traveled to Virginia to spend a weekend getting certified to teach HypnoBirthing®, The Mongan Method. We had a small class, four of us total. One woman was a Certified Nurse Midwife. I didn't even know what that was. She explained it to me and it sounded so right. I think of midwives at a birth like a lifeguard when people are swimming; they will jump in and save you but only if you're drowning and in need of assistance.

We spent the whole weekend deep in hypnosis, practicing techniques and learning about birthing in a healthy, positive way, free of fear and preconditioned beliefs.

I brought the skills and my new certification back to my hometown and began offering classes. Right away the classes filled. Expectant Moms were picking up what I was putting down! Many positive, empowering births came out of my teachings. Around this time, I had also started teaching yoga at the same studio where I attended my prenatal yoga classes.

I very quickly went from teaching gentle classes to adding on my own prenatal yoga offerings, as well as restorative yoga workshops. There was a woman who came to a HypnoBirthing series and my weekly prenatal yoga classes. We had a special connection, though I do connect with all the women who are seeking more conscious, empowering experiences of birth. This woman in particular, a fellow "birth nerd," asked me if I would be her Birth Doula. It was something I knew I wanted to do but just hadn't really put it out there yet.

A Birth Doula is a companion who is present for the laboring mom and her birth companion during birth to offer support on all levels-emotional, mental, physical, spiritual.

Of course I agreed to accompany her to her labor and birth! Hellz Yeah!!

When you're living your **Divine Assignment**, once you *listen to the whispers, trust your intuition, and take inspired action*, it all lines up beautifully!

I was sooooo thankful to be living on purpose. I had the luxury of knowing what I wanted to do in order to serve, create a positive lasting impression, fully embrace my ability to "work" in this sense, and make money doing it all!

I was still keeping up with my own yoga practice and in addition to teaching a couple nights a week, I was also attending classes as a student. The plan was to Keep Showing Up and it was working! I wasn't certified to teach yet, though I felt very confident in my offerings and in my classes. My devoted students were increasing in numbers which reflected back to me that I was doing something right.

I decided after a year and a half of teaching yoga that maybe I should jump through the hoop and get certified. I knew obtaining certification would add more clout to my presence and I was eager to learn MORE of this ancient practice.

I researched programs and ultimately decided on registering for a 200-hr yoga teacher training at Kripalu Center. This was where my first yoga instructor had been certified from so the style was familiar to me. I committed to the 2x12 format; Two twelve day stretches to completely immerse in all things yoga!!

This was one of the most life changing experiences I've ever had. The center is amazing, all on its own. Then layer on some deep soul searching, tearing down the walls of ourselves, revealing our true divinity, learning all about these practices that are thousands of years old (beyond the newest addition to yoga-the asana or poses) and top it off with some major confidence boosters, we were SHINING when we all graduated the program.

I had the grace of going through this program with one of my soul sisters who I first met when I worked at a childcare center. I was 17 years old, still in high school. This woman and I were friends then and had sort of lost touch throughout the years. It was truly divine that we both ended up at this retreat center in the Berkshire Mountains of Massachusetts at the same time, enrolled in the same training with 50+ souls in our class. We got to experience this intensity together yet separate. She is a friend for life, always a grounding sounding board.

* * *

In this program, I had the meaning of "Keep Showing Up" drilled into me. I felt excited about the start of the program, keep showing up. I felt overwhelmed by the content of the ENTIRE 200hr program, keep showing up. I felt intense sadness, grief, confusion over the death of my former self as we moved through the passion of the program, keep showing up. I was exhausted by daily 630am sadhana (devotional practice in the form of a 75-minute yoga class), morning programs, afternoon programs, evening sadhana (asana) practices, and all other obligations we had to keep up with, just keep showing up. I was missing my young boys and my family, keep showing up. I wanted to support my friends going through their own experiences of the program, keep showing up. We had our six-week break between the 2x12, keep showing up. We all returned to dance, play, move, learn, practice new skills, keep showing up. One of our sisters in the program shared her story of great loss that happened during our break, we all mourned with her, keep showing up. My (ex) husband broke his jaw while I was there wrapping up my training, just keep showing up.

See the theme?? No matter what comes up in life, we keep showing up. No matter the feelings, the responses, the patterns/tendencies/ingrained habits we keep showing up.

Just keep showing up and doing your best!! Your best will inevitably look different day to day because we are all so dynamic!! And that's a beautiful thing.

Obtaining my 200 hour yoga certification from Kripalu was a pivotal experience in my life. It was an accomplishment that felt greater than my four-year degree in Psychology. It demanded more of me. It called on me to take a much deeper look at myself on sooooo many layers of my being. I loved the emphasis on spirituality, on the awareness of how multi-dimensional we are as spiritual beings having a human experience. I loved how it wasn't about the asana, the yoga poses; they are a very small part of what yoga truly is. Yoga is a lifestyle. It's maintaining an expanded awareness of our consciousness. It's trusting that there is a greater plan in motion. It is deep healing on a soul level. This is what I carry with me to this day.

* * *

Back home, I continued offering yoga classes, empowering birthing classes, doing energy healing as a Reiki practitioner, and "working" as a birth doula. After that first birth I was invited to, I knew without a shadow of a doubt that this was part of my path. I remember my first client, the fellow birth nerd, looking me in my eyes and saying "Kara, you were made for this."

Being so grounded in myself through my yoga practice, meditations and motherhood I easily supported many women through their own empowering experiences of birth. I love holding space for others to be themselves and step into their power. This comes very naturally to me. Having been through my own healing from the childhood sexual abuse, the other betrayals against my body, navigating a marriage to my boy's dad, standing in my own place of empowerment, living my soul's purpose provided me the amazing opportunity to be present with others during their times of need.

During this time, I had begun "unschooling" my boys. This is a philosophy of child-led learning, similar to Montessori. We had the joy and luxury of becoming aware of what my boys were naturally interested in and researching to our hearts' content! Topics included dinosaurs, any reptiles and amphibians, reading books about anything and everything, doing art projects and exploring creativity, going to our local zoo, science center, museum of play, etc. We were always going on adventures. I was able to be present and available for my boys, giving them the stable foundation I know they needed to grow into secure, confident adults.

* * *

I was with my boy's dad for twelve years, married for seven. We grew up together. We were both new at relationships when we got together at nineteen and had no idea how to handle conflict or wtf "repair" meant. Throughout the course of our time together we had a lot of ups and downs. The dynamic was very tumultuous which led to a lot of damage within the relationship. Broken trust, respect dwindling, love lost. Once all that is gone it's very difficult to get it back. We were stuck in the lower vibrational states of shame, fear, blame, frustration, disappointment, etc.

I didn't know it at the time but I had major nervous system dysregulation. We would fight and I would leave. We would fight and I would leave. Repeat.

It got to a point within the relationship when it was time to move on. Choosing to break up our nuclear family was one of the most difficult decisions I've ever had to make. Intuitively I knew it was time.

Months after making this decision, I moved with our boys into a two-bedroom apartment. I had never lived in an apartment complex before. I didn't have my dog. I was alone there with them. I had no other choice than to Keep Showing Up. And I did. Every single day.

We still unschooled for the first year after we moved out. In this time I was able to get my feet back under me, grieve and mourn the loss of the life I thought I'd have. I grew up in a broken home and I remember the feeling of wanting to have kids young so I could have a family. This dream was shot down....or so I thought.

I was devoted to being a mom to my boys, I had no interest in dating or opening my heart back up on that front. I chose to stay focused on motherhood and my growing career.

I threw myself into my yoga practice any and every chance I got. For sure: every night, after I put my boys to bed I would unroll my mat, turn the lights down, listen to music and flow. However my body needed to move, it would move. Through this movement, I cried a lot. Our physical body holds trauma and sadness. In moving intuitively I was holding space for myself to release the stress that had been built up. This was my own **somatic healing** and practice **regulating my nervous system**, bringing myself back to the calm, safe, grounded space was crucial to my healing from the divorce and from all the other traumas this pain triggered.

* * *

After a certain amount of mourning I got back to focusing on growing my birth business. I was still teaching yoga, childbirth education classes, and taking birth doula clients. I reached a point when I realized I wanted to have a more positive impact. I wanted to do my part to change the culture of birth in our country so I vowed to become a Midwife (like the woman I met at the HypnoBirthing facilitators training) so I could play more of an active role in women's birthing. This meant I needed to be a nurse, to become a Certified NURSE Midwife. So…back to school I went!

Nursing school was hard. VERY hard. One of the most challenging things I've ever done, and I am no stranger to challenging things! During this time, I grew tremendously. I relied on my family a lot for support on all levels. I was also on welfare, receiving monthly food stamps and government funded health insurance. This was difficult for me, though I knew it was a temporary situation. My boys wanted to enroll in Karate. The monthly tuition seemed enormous at the time. Thankfully, the manager there let both my guys take classes in exchange for my cleaning services. While they practiced katas, I cleaned bathrooms and entryways. Humbling, to say the least. After three intense years, I passed nursing school and got my degree!! Kara Karaoguz RN!! Woot!

* * *

During this time I had begun dating a man I had dated before, back when I was fifteen. He was the one person I always wondered about, the "what if" kinda person. I feel like everyone has the one person whom they always feel connected to, always wonder what would have happened if things worked out.

When we were spending time together initially, he didn't want to commit. I refused to take no for an answer because I knew how strong our connection was. Through all my yoga and other spiritual practices, I have cultivated a very strong intuition and I am naturally guided by it. This I knew: We were meant to be together.

Despite his reluctance, I cast a spell on him. A love spell. Sorcery and witchcraft-type cast a spell!! I did!!

And it worked! I let it all go and months later he came back to me, begging to spend time together. As soon as I let my guard down, we were inseparable. Things moved fast and within a few short months of being a couple, we moved in together.

And, ya know, the funny thing about red flags is: You see them and choose to turn a blind eye. Because I tend to focus on the positive and only see the good in people (much to my detriment at times), I opted to focus on the potential and all the possibility *we* had going for us.

I realized early on that I had soul contracts and agreements with his soul. There were lessons to be learned. It dawned on us that we were Twin Flames (TF). The TF mirrors back to you all your shadows, hurts and vulnerabilities so you can heal them.

For me, being in a relationship dynamic with this person showed me my deep core wounds of abandonment, fears of rejection though I really thought I had done enough work on myself after my divorce to not repeat this pattern. Apparently not. Again, I had major nervous system dysregulation. I would feel threatened and go to one of the Four F's (Fight, Flight, Fawn, Freeze), as we all do. You'll learn more about this in Part II.

Though we loved each other very much, felt a divine connection bigger than us in our ego-driven 3D earthly bodies, we just couldn't make it work. More on 3rd Dimension vs 5th Dimension thinking in Part II. We would have conflict and majorly trigger each other. Now I know that it was all by design. It was all to show me what I get to heal in this life time so as to not repeat the karmic cycle.

Spoiler Alert: After years of trying to make it work, I realized it was a no-go. More on this to come. During the demise of this relationship I became aware of attachment styles and how different dynamics play out, such as co-dependency. This is so classic and often a byproduct of having a history of trauma or abuse. The core wounds of shame, guilt, distrust, fear of rejection and fear of abandonment rear their ugly heads when we feel threatened. The autonomic nervous system fires off with physiological responses, our default insecure attachment styles show up and basically we're fucked.

There is hope. There is a way to unlearn and relearn new patterns of behavior, new responses to threats within the relationship, and reprogram so as to repair in a healthy, productive way. Part II is jammmmm packed with all the things to get you on the right track.

As an Empath and Healer, I soooo badly wanted to "fix" this relationship and be able to grow together. It took me a long time to realize that it's not my job to make him want to grow, expand, evolve, or ascend with me. What I really wanted was for us to each do our own work and meet together with new understandings of our wounding. That didn't happen. As an Intuitive Life Coach, guiding those through their own healing is in my blood. I know that I am able to activate a frequency in others then it is up to them to get curious and do their own work.

Unfortunately, I was taught from a young age that love and abuse can co-exist. This ingrained belief allowed me to energetically attract this dynamic twice. I realized if I don't do my own deeply healing inner work then I will continue to attract this dynamic. So I set out to heal the shit out of myself.

* * *

Something else I factored into the formation of my beliefs was an important concept around emotional availability. Or rather, in this case, emotional UNavailability. Within the dynamic with the TF, I so badly wanted to be a priority, I wanted to seen, heard, validated. These were not things that he was capable of. One reason was his default insecure attachment style. Another reason was the presence of his ego and shadow self running the show. The question that haunted me was: "How could I be okay being with someone so emotionally unavailable to me?!"

The response from my Higher Self was to look at my upbringing and find the similarities. I've never been one to mask a problem, hoping for a long-term solution. I understand the importance of identifying the root cause and doing the healing work from the ground up. Remarkably, it all started to make sense.

My parents got divorced when I was eighteen months old. My (older) brother and I lived with my mom Rebecca and we saw our dad every other weekend. For her, as a single mom on a nurse's salary with little to no child support from my dad, she was spread thin. As I have grown older I see how emotionally unavailable both my parents were. Not in a malicious, purposefully neglectful way; more so because they were too caught up in their own pain. In this healing journey, a big part of finding forgiveness is understanding that our parents are human too with flaws of their own. This revelation was never coming from a place of blame, more from a place of compassion in an effort to understand my upbringing.

My maternal grandmother, Josephine or "Nini" as I called her, was the one who was more present in my childhood. She was a stable, loving force and I clung to that. She instilled the concept of being a homemaker into my bones. I am certain that I can create a home out of any environment I live in, thanks to her.

Before Josephine started a family of her own, she was an RN. She had aspirations of being a cadet nurse in the Army during WWII. Once she married my grandfather and they welcomed their firstborn, she committed herself to a life as a homemaker. Classic mid-century family structure. My grandfather, Anthony, was the Hospital Administrator at our local hospital for nearly twenty years. My grandparents moved to the area from Pittsburgh, PA, when my mom was a senior in high school so he could take the CEO position. Thanks to my grandparent's prestige, they established a distinguished reputation for our family. Since my grandfather was on the Board of Directors, he was very close with other prominent families in the area. Josephine was always composed and self-assured; she had a regal presence to her. She was magnetic and I loved being around her.

My dad, Ergun, is fifteen years older than my mom. He came to America from Turkey in the 1960's on a student visa and never returned. My whole paternal side of the family lives there still. I've gotten the chance to travel to Turkey twice, when I was 16 and 19. Despite fighting against going I had the most amazing experiences seeing the lands, basking in the culture, eating the foods, and spending time with my family! It's funny how the things we resist the most (out of fear) often turn out to be some of the most incredible, life-changing experiences.

* * *

After graduating from nursing school at age thirty-five, I was working as an RN at a hospital getting in my obligatory one year of "med-surg". This is a medical-surgical unit where everybody and their mother comes in for every illness under the sun. As a nurse in this position, you get a TON of exposure and experience with it all. I was working three twelve hour shifts a week. It sounds do-able but it FEELS draining.

It was in this time I came to see my Empathic, clairsentient qualities screaming loud for me to listen. In all the interactions with my co-workers, my patients, their families, every single person I could feel their feelings, processing deeply all the stimuli I was taking in. Each interaction took a little piece of me and by the time I got home, I had nothing left to give my family. Empaths and Highly Sensitive People (as you know) can feel the emotions of others and we tend to take on their pain as a way to help heal them. We are like energetic sponges.

I was moving from an extremely unaware, unempowered state in regards to this superpower. I had no protective practices in place. I transitioned to an RN Pediatric Palliative Care Case Manager position at a home care agency, driving all over a large county in and around the city of Rochester, NY. I visited families of my pediatric patients and could feel very intensely what each and every one of them were experiencing. At this point, I was attempting to protect myself though I was still utterly exhausted after a shift.

Realizing that this position is more draining than uplifting, I decided I needed to get back to my soul assignment and what lights me up: my birth services. I cut back my hours and began energetically attracting birth clients. This filled my love tank for a short period of time. Then it became very clear that I was being called to honor my original assignment: to help survivors heal from abuse. Remember, this was why I went to school initially, locking in my degree in Psychology. And now, coming full circle, it hit me that I needed to get back to supporting others on their healing journey.

Experiencing a subtle shift in my own energy, I began to attract life coaching clients. I hadn't even created a website or announced it to my growing communities on social media when I started getting messages from strangers asking if we could work together: "I'm not even sure if you do this but my intuition is leading me to you so I had to listen."

Why, yes, yes I do coach others through difficult transitions, onto healing and experiencing more fullness and satisfaction in life! Hell yes. As joyful as all this felt, things in my life were about to take a turn for the worse.

CHAPTER 4

The Beet* Goes On

"Grief, I've learned, is really just love. It's all the love you want to give but cannot. All of that unspent love gathers up in the corners of your eyes, the lump in your throat and that hollow part of your chest. Grief is just love with no place to go." -Jamie Anderson

As mentioned before, things with the Twin Flame (TF) did not work out. But we had still been living together trying our darnedest to live in harmony. After an abrupt split from him, my boys and I moved out to have our own space. It was a really sad, tough decision to make. Once the bad times start to outweigh the good, something's gotta

give. I was living on my own, with my boys and our awesome dog
Koda Bear, my German Shepherd BFF. I was still working as a
pediatric nurse. I was taking birth doula clients, teaching childbirth
education, and building an Intuitive Life Coaching practice. There
were a lot of moving parts. My relationship status remained unstable.
The TF and I were on/off, on/off, primarily due to our intense love
for one another and our shoddy boundaries when it came to our
attempts to stay apart.

I was so in love with coaching others and in doing so, I felt energized
and alive guiding clients into their own empowerment. It's a re-birth
of self and clearly I LOVE birth!! Whether its the physical act of
giving birth or the spiritual, metaphysical act of rebirth, a new
version of the self, I am here for it!!

When you are living your purpose, the "work" feels very energizing.
You naturally take inspired action that is aligned with your mission.

* * *

In early 2019, my firecracker 93-year old grandmother started having
serious health issues. Her blood pressure was very high, which
majorly disrupted her system. Macular degeneration of the eyes was
kicked into high gear and she was legally blind, only seeing shadows,

unable to make out even the food was on her plate. She had constant pains down her legs from nerves in her back. My grandfather, who we called "Pappap," crossed over in 2014. All four of her sisters and many friends had passed. She was weak and exhausted all the time and couldn't wait for 6pm to roll around so she could go get into bed, watch TV and fall asleep.

Growing up, her home was the most stable, comforting place I had. Her presence was strong and available, and I could always go to Nini's house to calm down when I was upset. We had a tight-knit, Italian family. My grandparents had been married 65+ years. My mom, brother and I lived right around the corner from my grandparents. My aunts lived 30 minutes away. My uncle was also in town after living most of his life in Florida and Santa Fe; he came back home as my grandparents were aging. We spent holidays and special occasions together at her home. I spent many days there with Nini, watching Dr. Phil, Judge Judy, murder mysteries that would always stay with me way too long (hello, Empath!), or just listening to music as we talked.

She had many token phrases that our family dubbed "Nini-isms," among them "the show must go on" which illustrated the actress in her, always aware of the need to keep showing up. *She was also known to say "the beet goes on" when eating beets, double entendre intended. The undercurrent was to show up and do your best.

After many years contemplating, faced with her failing health and rapidly diminishing quality of life, she decided she no longer wanted to live. Her mind was made up. There was no way to talk her out of it. And why would we? This was her life and we all completely understood. The only joys she had left were sipping black coffee, taking a puff or two of her Camel non-filters, her scratch-off lotto tickets and hitting up the local racino once in a while to play the slots. She was tired.

So we got the ball rolling by talking to a palliative care doctor who told us that once Nini stopped eating and drinking she would be considered terminal. Typically, the only reason to go into hospice is if there is an illness with a prognosis of less than six months to live. She had no such prognosis. At the age of 93, she was just done with this life.

Her end-of-life, dying with dignity **vision** is actually a thing. So many older people are now taking their deaths into their own hands. It even has its own acronym: VSED which stands for voluntary stopping of eating and drinking. I believe its a much better route than withering away in a nursing home, just waiting for the grim reaper to come.

Leading up to her "fast," as she called it, I spent many days with her. I sat beside her while she called her remaining friends and shared her "good news" with them. They were all very tearful and appreciative of their friendship. She was a trailblazer. They knew that. I'm sure its part of what they all loved about her.

Anytime we would talk about her plan, I would cry. She would very matter-of-factly say: "Well Kara, I can't live forever!" One of the reasons I wanted to have kids at a young age was so they could meet and get to know my grandparents. My boys and I spent sooooo much time there. It was their second home as much as it was mine.

Nini's next step was to pick a date to stop eating and drinking. She picked my older son's 14th birthday as her last full meal. We always got together to celebrate birthdays in her home. It was a very hard dinner to get through. We hadn't told the boys exactly what was about to unfold.

I wanted them to be as prepared as possible while sparing them the details. So I told them that her days with us were numbered, but I didn't say much more. I would say "Nini is getting older, you know. We can't live forever," taking a page out of her book. They understood.

The morning after her last meal, on February 28, 2019, she enjoyed her last cup of coffee. Ever. I had taken a family medical leave from my nursing position so I could be present during this process.

Her "dream team," as we called ourselves, consisted of myself; my mom a retired RN with a 45-year career under her belt who came up from Key West, Florida; my aunts (my aunt's partner of 37 years was also an RN with many years of experience); and both my uncles: the one who was local, and one who joined us from Virginia.

The first day of her fast, Nini was in great spirits, so excited because she was actually doing this; it was really happening!! On the second day, she was still upbeat, donning the tiara she was known for wearing during celebrations. By the end of that day, however, and into the nest, she became very agitated and frustrated.

On the second day, we had Nini in a hospital bed in the family room because she thought she would want to be downstairs. The snow was falling outside so slowly, like we were all inside a snow globe that had just been shaken up. We had instrumental music playing for most of the day. It was very peaceful.

That evening she decided she wanted to be in her own bed so we slowly, deliberately escorted her up the stairs. I was on her left, elbows locked with her hand in mine, supporting her and giving her strength to walk "independently" from point A to point B. My uncle was on her right, doing much of the same. She had a sweet little shuffle because she was so weak. With her sense of humor very much intact, she said "boy it's a good thing there isn't a fire!" We all simultaneously laughed and cried, feeling such reverence for her sharp wit shining right through during this extraordinary experience.

After consulting with the doctor, we adjusted her hospice meds and as previously discussed with her, opted to keep her sedated. These were her wishes. As the strong women she had raised, we were honoring those wishes in every way possible.

We sat vigil bedside by her bedside around the clock. I went home at night to sleep then went right back over to Nini's first thing each morning. We were keeping a log of her meds, noting the dose and the time. We rotated her position often, bathed her, kept her mouth moistened. We rubbed medicated menthol lotion on her body to ease her itchiness from the morphine that was helping to keep her comfortable, free of pain, and slowing her breathing. We had music playing the entire day. Simon and Garfunkel, James Taylor, Andrea Bocelli all on repeat. We talked with each other in attempts to make this situation seem as normal as possible. Nini was no longer talking or awake.

On the fifth evening, my ex-husband went to the pharmacy for us to pick up a refill of her medication. We had no idea how long this would go on for. We had been told it could take 7-10 days. When he brought the prescription, he wanted to see her. She always loved him. Even when things were very difficult between us, she would always say, "Kara, he is the boy's dad. Be nice." She was a second grandmother to him, and he was a part of our family even though our relationship had changed shape.

When he entered the room with all of us standing around, welcoming in this new person to our protected, sacred space, he was taken aback. He put his hand to his mouth and fought back tears as he sat beside her. He said, "This is hard," which felt sobering to us all. We were so immersed and focused on our task: to keep the matriarch of our family comfortable as her soul prepared to leave her physical body. At the time, I didn't let myself think of the sadness or the resonance of doing this great deed for her. He had some time to say his goodbyes, then he left, heading home to our boys who were staying with him.

I left shortly thereafter and went home to seek some familiarity and comfort. I wanted to take a bath, and filled the tub as soon as I got home. When I had left them all 30 minutes prior, I told the family that if ANYTHING changed with Nini's breathing to let me know immediately. As I was soaking in the hot epsom salt water, trying to wash the stress away, my phone rang. It was my aunt.

"Did her breathing change?" I asked her.

After a short pause she said, "Honey, you better come back over here now."

"Is she okay? Is she gone?!" I asked, my thoughts starting to blur.

She repeated: "Just come over honey."

I got out of the tub, got dressed as fast as I could, raced over. I remember thinking while I was driving the 5 miles to her home: slow down, it's not gonna matter cuz she's gone.

When I got to the house, I ran inside and up the stairs to her room to find the dream team sitting around her body. She was gone. They had already dressed her in the angelic white satin nightie that she bought special for after she passed. She looked so peaceful. It was so crushing to know she was gone and that this was all over. The end of an era.

I shared the following essay two months after her death at Nini's celebration of life. During the planning, I was undecided about whether I would talk in her honor. The morning before the gathering, this all came through me in a rush. I believe it was channeled. I had been asking for her guidance about what to say:

" *"Nini" has been a second mother to me. Growing up, our mom worked full time as a single mom so we were at Nini and Pappap's a lot. Some of my earliest memories with Nini are of us playing cards. She taught us at a young age and would say she did so she would have someone to play cards with.*

She always provided stability and a safe place to land. I remember her always being so poised...as the leader of the pack. Our strong matriarch.

Among many other things, she taught me about making a home and the importance of sitting down together for mealtimes. Lunches were typically cold cuts from Casa Italiana, kept folded in their white paper secured with tape, fresh sliced provolone from a block, honey mustard or mayo (you pick), lettuce, pepperoncinis, bread and butter pickles, served on lightly toasted "nice bread" with a side of chips and fresh cut cantaloupe (or some other melon). Dinners were just as consistent. I could count on a delicious COLORFUL home cooked meal, with a side salad draped in oil and red wine vinegar with a dash of garlic salt at 5 o'clock every night.

My adolescent years were spent rebelling in any way I could. When looking back on this time, she would always say "If I had a gun, I would have shot her!"

She taught me to follow my intuition and always speak in honesty and integrity. She would say "I do not speak with forked tongue".

She had an insatiable thirst for knowledge, always curious about root words and derivatives. When I was a child she was always offering "language lessons" that included a new word, typically in another language that she would teach us. These lessons continued on to my boys, whom she absolutely loved and adored. One of my hopes in having children at a young age was to have them really KNOW Nini (& Pappap). I think we succeeded.

She was just as stable of a force in their lives as she was mine. My Nini and her home on Holiday Lane ("where every day is a holiday") was always a beacon. She was my rock. Someone I could always count on. No matter what. She always looked to see the good in people and if any of us weren't getting along she would say, "Now what's really going on?" searching below the surface for the root cause of the issue.

She made an indelible imprint on my life. I feel sooo blessed to have had her for all these years as an amazing, loving, intelligent grandmother. When I have grandchildren, they will call me "Nini"."

That was one of the hardest things I've ever had to do, second to testifying during my trial. Up until this point I had never felt such a scorching loss or missed someone every single day. But I was about to find out that the grieving process had only just begun.

KEEP SHOWING UP

CHAPTER 5

Cycle Breaker

"We repeat what we don't repair." Anonymous

No one talks about the amount of grief you may experience when breaking cycles, ending codependency, and leaving former versions of yourself behind. It is messy and painful, with tearful days full of deep sorrow and self loathing: "Why can't I just get the message??" Major cognitive dissonance.

Around the time of my grandmother's passing, the Twin Flame (TF) and I rekindled after having been off for months. He showed up at my door the day after she passed, saying he woke up knowing something had shifted. That's how connected we were.

What blows me away the most about myself is that I understood full well how much our relationship was a rollercoaster. It was unhealthy and toxic AF, yet I had the most difficult time pulling myself away from it. We cycled on and off for two years. **TWO YEARS**.

Things would be amazing for a short period of time and I would feel so much hope, just knowing we would end up together. I was so optimistic that we could heal the deep wounds we had, from generational trauma and our own lives, then ride off into the sunset together. But then, in the blink of an eye, it would all come crashing down, seemingly harder than ever before. Each time that happened, pieces of my heart shattered. Through this intense heartache I was also able to gain more insight into myself and the dynamic of the situation.

I had seen his potential from the very beginning, knowing all the good he had inside him. Time and again, I chose to overlook his shortcomings. Now, looking back, I could point the finger and blame him for all the things I feel he did to contribute to our demise. But let's be honest: There is no gain in playing that card.

One thing I know to be true about of taking **responsibility** for our actions is that the word itself conveys a lot. Response-Ability: our ability to respond. I value how my yoga practice provided me with equanimity. It gave me experience in responding instead of reacting to things that sent my nervous system into high gear.

There is a Viktor Frankl quote that I love so much and think of often:

"Between stimulus and response there is a space. In the space is our power to choose our response. In our response lies our growth and our freedom."

My asana practice lets me tap into this energy so I am able to be more reflective. I don't always succeed, but the intention is there. Work in progress. Just like I tell my clients: "It's all practice."

* * *

As part of my healing lifestyle and ongoing connection to Source, I turned the finger back to myself to determine how I was contributing to the unhealthy relationship dynamic. To see it for what it was: codependency. I am hesitant to use labels because they are so general. In Part II, I dismantle this dynamic so you can see how it may apply to you. There are many themes and overlapping concepts.

Through my healing process, the patterns have become crystal clear to me. I GET TO keep the conversation going around this topic. It affects so many people.

I was also determined to become aware of my own core wounding of shame, inferiority, fear of rejection and fear of abandonment. I believe in going back to the root of the problem to rectify the situation or reshape the limiting beliefs.

I finally accepted that my self-worth was being compromised by staying in the relationship with the man I thought was my Twin Flame. Maybe he was. I go into more detail about Soul Mates, Twin Flames, Life Partners, Soul Contracts, Karmic Bonds and the like in Part II. When you have to abandon your own needs just to have someone else's love, it cannot be good.

I also realized I had dysfunction in my nervous system every time I felt threatened in the relationship. I'm referring to an emotionally unsafe dynamic. Harsh words being spoken. Accusations. Not feeling protected against outside threats, like a very difficult, vindictive ex-partner of his. Not feeling the same love I gave him echoed back to me.

What really shifted my thinking was learning about Attachment Theory as it applies to adult relationships. I had learned from studies in psychology how important our formative years were; this is when attachment styles are shaped. When threatened, we default to an insecure style if the foundation of the relationship is not stable.

It was a perfect storm of his core wounding mixed with mine and we set each other off with such intensity. Major triggers. Through this relationship I came to realize that our **triggers are our treasures**. They reflected back to me where my own healing was needed. I very clearly saw my core wounds, my autonomic nervous system dysregulation, my insecure anxious attachment that came out in full force when I didn't feel safe. I get into all this in Part II.

Our triggers are not caused by the present day situation but are rooted in a trauma. How that trauma was dealt with determines a lot about how our lives unfold. I'm speaking mostly of core wounds like shame and guilt, feeling inferior, insignificant or not enough, feeling unworthy, unseen, unheard or unloved, fearing rejection or abandonment. Combine that with defense mechanisms and no repair from conflict, you get a really toxic relationship. When the trauma resurfaces in adult dynamics, it can to be healed through safe relationships.

"You don't have relationship problems, you have childhood problems that are disguising themselves as relationship problems." -Raz Soos

Thankfully I discovered the antidote to all these unhealthy patterns: self-love mastery. Lots of work around radical acceptance and boundaries, inner child work and ongoing learning and practice. And an increase in self worth. Know Your Worth. In addition, I've learned to accept my shadow self, my perceived flaws, no longer tolerating negative self talk. I allow myself to fully be myself, unapologetically me! I've chosen to focus more on gratitude, staying as high vibe as possible, and my growing online coaching business.

I continue to flow through this life as an Intuitive Self Healer and a Life Coach, supporting my clients on very similar tasks. It took me long enough to "get it" and I am so happy to write that I do now. I celebrate as much as possible, from the essential oils I diffuse each morning and throughout the day to the genuine connections I get to share with others. In person or virtually, big and small, they're one and the same.

But the *grieving process* was quite a ride. Five months before my grandmother passed, I had moved out from living w TF. We proceeded to ride the rollercoaster of emotions for another year-plus. <u>Denial</u> is very real; I didn't want to see the truth of this death for a long time. When a relationship has so much hurt, if both parties aren't willing to stretch themselves outside their comfort zones and consciously unlearn and relearn new ways of coping, navigating, showing up, then it's doomed. <u>Anger</u> is said to be "sad's bodyguard." It is energizing, hot and fiery, and it allowed me to protect myself at times. Anger fueled my fitness many times. <u>Bargaining</u> went on for over two years. How bad did I want things to work out?? So bad. How much did we both bargain with one another thinking: "This time will be different."? Wayyy too many times to count. <u>Depression</u> is agonizing and very painful. I am typically an optimistic person, so moving through this phase of grief was VERY uncomfortable for me. I spent entire days crying, exhausted from the heartache, unable to reach out to any of my supports, not wanting to bother them, embarrassed and ashamed that this was all STILL going on. I felt very isolated in this Lone Wolf phase. Finally shifting to <u>Acceptance</u>, I gather strength from a Matt Kahn quote:

"Despite how open, peaceful, and loving you attempt to be, people can only meet you as deeply as they've met themselves. This is the heart of clarity."

And this Osho quote:

TRUTH

· · · · · · · · · ● ● ● ● ● ● ● ● ● ● ● ● · · · · · · · ·

@kara_karaoguz

"IF YOU LOVE YOURSELF, YOU LOVE
OTHERS. IF YOU HATE YOURSELF,
YOU HATE OTHERS. BECAUSE IN
RELATIONSHIP WITH OTHERS...
*the other is nothing
but a mirror.*"

~OSHO

www.karakaraoguz.com

Basically, it's really not about you. It never was.

How we show up for others is a reflection of our own inner landscape.

How we show love or withhold, how we show affection or not, if we communicate effectively or not...All of this reveals the inner states.

I love the quotes above because they have helped me understand why certain people haven't loved me back the way I have loved them.

It's not about you. It's their shit. You get to decide if you're okay with that, then act accordingly.

* * *

As part of rebuilding my own structures, I am aware of the impact I get to have on my community. Leaving my pediatric RN position the fall after my grandmother passed gave me great freedom to explore and grow my life coaching business. The concept of rebirth continues to present itself, as we are all in various stages of destruction and re-creation of self. Let yourself fall, crumble, shatter then rebuild stronger than ever before. It can be done. It powerfully leads you into your next chapter of life.

CHAPTER 6

Soul Purpose

"Don't ask what the world needs. Ask yourself what makes you come alive, then go do that, because what the world needs is people who have come alive."

-Howard Thurman

From very early on, knowing that I wanted to get my degree in psychology to help survivors heal from abuse was a gift that came out of the turmoil I experienced in my childhood and adolescence. Then the traumatic birth experience with my first son opened me to the concept of working as a birth professional to empower women. My birth doula work is so meaningful to me, as is teaching about the natural, physiological birth philosophy of HypnoBirthing.

Obtaining my nursing degree and getting to work as a birth assistant with the home birth midwives, I experience the uninhibited beauty of birth, as nature intends. We get to support, encourage, reassure the laboring mom while engaging in casual conversation, feeling the breeze of the warm summer air drift in through open windows. We get to ensure their safety and provide an empowering experience of birth to the mama, allowing that confidence and inner glow to spill into her motherhood.

Getting back to my Divine Assignment to support clients through the deeply healing inner work feels so aligned. Whether I'm working with my 1:1 clients or those in my group programs, together we release the false self for the purpose of their souls ascension so they can manifest a life beyond their WiLdeSt dreams.

This "work" is so right for me on a very deep level. This is what I am here to do. I am certain.

* * *

Leaving my pediatric palliative care position meant leaving behind the sick babies, children, and families I worked very closely with. I loved the patients I had the honor of providing care to, but the actual job left me EXTREMELY drained each day.

I saw babies born with congenital cardiac anomalies awaiting heart repairs to function "normally." Babies and kids with feeding difficulties who needed G-tubes (gastrostomy tubes straight to the belly) or NG-tubes (naso-gastric tubes, through the nose to the stomach) just to get their nutrition. Babies and kids with tracheostomies, on ventilators, needing supplemental oxygen to breathe. Kids with cancer receiving chemotherapy, who needed lab draws in the home so an oncologist could assess their bloodwork. Moms and babies who needed support with lactation, wound care, burn care... These are just some patients I would see in the home. It feels heavy, right?? It definitely kept things in perspective. You think you're having a bad day or some personal struggle then you go see a little sweetheart with cancer who is crying during the visit, asking, "Why does everything have to be so hard?"

Yeah. Everything is relative.

Despite having an awareness of the intuitive clairsentient abilities I possess, this job really drilled home how much of an Empath I am. I can sense and feel the emotions and energies of others. Because of my work, it felt like I had very little to give my family when I got home from a day seeing patients. Being an "Unaware" Empath, I was able to take on the emotions of those I came into contact with. To know how they were feeling without them even having to say it. Each encounter left me increasingly drained. I vowed to become an "Empowered" Empath; if I didn't, I wouldn't last long with any of my calls to serve.

* * *

Leaving nursing to focus fully on life coaching was energizing. It was a terrifying leap to take, leaving the security of my nursing job, though I am so glad I did it! When we honor the call to our Divine Assignment, we feel enthusiastic and on FIRE! This also gave me freedom in my days to get out much more often in nature to ground myself and recharge my batteries. My favorite adventures are day trips hiking with my dog, preferably around waterfalls. There are quite a few state parks near me and we now get to explore them often.

Going out into nature was the most soothing practice I could do for myself through my years of grieving, coming to terms with the end of the life I thought I'd be living. Taking hot epsom salt baths came in a close second! I also need to move my body daily as part of my healing lifestyle. Working out, lifting weights, practicing yoga, sitting for meditation...all practices I need for my own mental health. These are necessary for me to stay balanced and emotionally regulated. I know myself enough to understand that these practices are staples in my life.

Through my own healing, I have come to see how important it is to incorporate self-love practices into each day; the little things add up to the big things.

Growing an online coaching business has been so much fun. When I realized my direction in life, my first step was to hire a business coach to assist me in streamlining the process. Since that first coach, I have continually worked with a mentor/guide/coach in some capacity so I can keep moving the needle forward with my healing and my business. Growing my online biz while living in alignment with my soul's purpose has taken an immense amount of trust and courage. I'm here for it all!

Through the grief and extreme heartache, I was able to follow my heart, continuing to grow, expand, evolve, ascend in this lifetime. Some beautiful lessons I have gained are Keep showing up. Be here, now. Live with **INTENTION**.

Through this intense healing journey, I had to put my own puzzle pieces together. I saw therapists who had no idea what I was experiencing or why. I felt misguided. This led to more confusion, shame, and frustration. I was determined to crack the code so I dug deep and starting bringing many different concepts together. These include psychological perspectives, physiological approaches, and of course, my own style of spirituality that is the undercurrent of all I do. Common themes I was seeing with my clients and group programs centered around these topics as well. As we move on to Part II, you'll see how these concepts and lessons fit into your own life. Remember, it's okay to take breaks as you move through the content. Listen to your body and take the time you need. And whatever you do: Keep. Showing. Up. xo

PART II

THE LESSONS: DO THE WORK

ARE YOU READY TO SWITCH GEARS (MENTALLY) AND
START APPLYING NEW PRACTICES TO YOUR LIFE??

Chapter 7

First Things First

"Awakening is not changing who you are, but discharging who you are not." -Deepak Chopra

Lesson 1: Grounding Practices

Here we go!! Before we dig into the meat of these exercises, I want to arm you with some worthwhile grounding practices to help support you as you move through the lessons.

There may be times when you feel you hit a wall with doing this work, when you feel like you shut down or don't want to keep going. Trust that this is part of the process. Keep Showing Up. Honor your resistance. Don't push yourself too hard, but find a healthy way to continue to move forward with your reflections and ever-increasing self-awareness.

Here is a list of ten highly-effective grounding practices when you need a break. Maybe you realize you have to step away for a hot minute to support your own processing of the information. If that's the case, that's OKAY!! You will integrate the lessons in your own time.

Check it, check it out:

1. Bring your awareness to THIS MOMENT. All is well. Right now.
2. Feel your feet under you. Allow the soles of both feet to be in contact with the floor/ground, slide forward and back and stay with the sensations.
3. Soften your eyes and facial muscles; this level of relaxation sets the tone for the rest of your body.
4. Place the tip of your tongue on the roof of your mouth behind the top front teeth
5. Inside mouth, make circles with the tip of your tongue on the roof of your mouth. Now, switch directions.
6. Check in with your breathing. Notice the natural in/out rhythm of your breaths (see Lesson 3). Try to slow your breathing down, lengthening the exhalation. I like a simple 1:2 ratio: Inhale for a three count, exhale for a six count. Or inhale for a four count, exhale for eight. I also really like a simple 4, 6 breath. Read on for description.
7. Take a walk, run, or other activity to discharge negative energy that may be stirred up.

8. Dance to really awesome music (whatever that means to you!! I like '90s hip hop ;))

9. Make "I Dream of Jeanie" arms: Put your hands on either shoulder, squeeze arms from shoulders to elbows, up and down.

10. Place your hands on your heart and ask yourself: What do I need right now? Tune in and meet your needs. Cultivate trust in yourself!

Lesson 2: Re-phrasing

As you move through this content, keep in mind that you will be un-learning and re-learning a lot. This restructuring process requires a conscious effort. Using a technique called "re-phrasing," you will practice a new way of using your words. Our thoughts and words shape our reality. Read on...

Two worthy re-phrasing mentions:

1. "Until now"

Use this phrase as you are purposefully shifting your thought patterns, beliefs, ingrained structures and habits. Be committed to this process and give yourself grace. We get "stuck" or set in our ways. When we realize something is no longer serving us, it's time to change.

Through the change, allow yourself to acknowledge how you **used** to show up by adding "until now" when stating your previous reality.

For example: "I have a hard time putting myself first...until now." Or "I look to others for love and neglect my own needs...until now." You are consciously co-creating a new reality. It's a practice. I believe in you.

2. "I get to"

Anytime you say "I have to" or "I need to," substitute the phrase "I get to." Your actions and choices are deliberate. When we speak in the old way, it feels more like a burden. There is a heaviness to "I have to..." There is desperation to "I need to..."

You GET TO decide how you show up. This phrase welcomes in your higher self, what is best for the greater good of all. It is an honor and a privilege to be the best version of yourself. You get to follow your heart. You get to be around people you love. You get to let love in. You get to enjoy your job. You get to change lives. You get to be kind.

Lesson 3: Pranayama aka Breath Work

So, My Love, it's this easy...break up patterns of breathing, break up patterns of thought. Period.

Accessing the breath will help you get ahead of your anxiety and play more of an active role in not letting it rule the roost. It is important to keep the breath moving in and out through the nose; you'll feel more grounded this way. Also, when you are breathing in, expand your belly, make it get big, then on your exhale, let it recede, draw your navel in towards your spine. This is huge.

Here's a simple practice to try right now:
- Keeping the breath in and out through the nose
- Expand your belly each time you breathe in
- Take a deep breath IN and count to 4 in your mind (when you get to 4, your lungs just about at their max capacity)
- Then slowly, effortlessly, let your exhalation spill out of the nose for a 6 count (same pace as in breath count)
- Drawing your belly in, forcing all the air out
- Repeat 4-6x
- Notice how you feel

If you are interested in more advanced breath work, reach out and I'll guide you.

In Yoga, one of the eight limbs is called Pranayama. Prana, meaning life force, and Ayama, meaning to stretch or expand. This practice is the manipulation of your breath to gain access to your inner world. It's dope. Try it!

I won't get into the eight limbs of yoga here. Trust me that they are significant and keep us connected to our spirituality. I encourage your own inquiry into yoga.

Lesson 4: Root Down to Rise Up

Above all else, you MUST know yourself. If you don't know who you are, no one else will either! You won't ever truly experience genuine, deep, meaningful connections with others. You will feel a disconnect from your emotions or from different situations. It will feel like something is off, or something is missing. You may experience a void, emptiness or pit in your stomach. This will be your reality until you make the choice to Do The Work and get to know yourself like never before. It isn't easy but it will be worth it. A quote I love is:

"When you want something you've never had, you have to do something you've never done".

In asana practice, it is vital to create a strong foundation for the poses on the mat. The concept of rooting down means building the pose from the ground up, in proper alignment. From that stability, you're able to rise up and expand out. When you move from a place of stability, you move from a place of strength. When you move from a place of strength you then have choice and power. In yoga and in life. Don't ever forget that!

In terms of our lives, root down in who you are. Truly know yourself in authenticity. Then all interactions with others are more genuine and meaningful. Then rise up into your fullest expression of self.

A great starting point is to establish a **Sacred Morning Practice**. I have written a Spiritual Guide to Living With Intention, going into great detail about morning, daily, and evening practices to best support you in Living With Intention. Intention is everything; without intention, your actions may feel empty and meaningless. When we have intention, we have more of a purpose.

The Sacred Morning Practice consists of your "morning care" routine: practices that are consistent, demonstrate self-love, and are hygienic in nature. This may include writing, planning, grounding/opening your vessel to your purpose, movement of some sort. Include positive affirmations/I am statements, and personal development reading or pulling an oracle card for the day. This daily practice helps connect you to your intuition, which is ultimately your soul speaking through you.

Lesson 5: Become the Witness
THIS. IS. WHAT. IT. IS. ALL. ABOUT.

"The highest spiritual practice is self-observation without judgment"

Swami Kripalu

I was first exposed to the concept of "witness consciousness" during my yoga teacher training in 2010 at Kripalu. You GET to practice observing yourself without judgment, sort of as a passenger along for the ride. You GET to **become the witness** of your thoughts, reactions, interactions, etc. This is how change happens. By slowing down, watching your thoughts, pausing, taking time to respond instead of react...that is where the MAGIC happens!!

It is necessary to stay soft, relaxed and breathe through the spiritual birthing of the new you during life transitions. The practice of meditation and stillness allows you to Get Quiet, often....

LISTEN<—>SILENT

(Same letters)

Lesson 6: Energetic Beings

Earlier in the book, I mentioned 3D emotional states. Here is a longer explanation of that theory:

We all emit a frequency and carry our own vibrations. These can change based on our emotions. There are some graphics that depict each emotion and its associated frequency measured in hertz. I have not actually measured them myself, so I won't list the hertz numbers here. According to this scale, however, the negative emotions are measured at lower vibrations ("low vibe") while positive ones are higher ("high vibe").

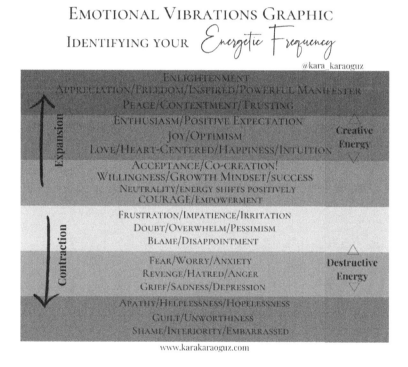

EMOTIONAL VIBRATIONS GRAPHIC
IDENTIFYING YOUR *Energetic Frequency*
@kara_karaoguz

ENLIGHTENMENT
APPRECIATION/FREEDOM/INSPIRED/POWERFUL MANIFESTER
PEACE/CONTENTMENT/TRUSTING
ENTHUSIASM/POSITIVE EXPECTATION
JOY/OPTIMISM
LOVE/HEART-CENTERED/HAPPINESS/INTUITION
ACCEPTANCE/CO-CREATION!
WILLINGNESS/GROWTH MINDSET/SUCCESS
NEUTRALITY/ENERGY SHIFTS POSITIVELY
COURAGE/EMPOWERMENT
FRUSTRATION/IMPATIENCE/IRRITATION
DOUBT/OVERWHELM/PESSIMISM
BLAME/DISAPPOINTMENT
FEAR/WORRY/ANXIETY
REVENGE/HATRED/ANGER
GRIEF/SADNESS/DEPRESSION
APATHY/HELPLESSNESS/HOPELESSNESS
GUILT/UNWORTHINESS
SHAME/INFERIORITY/EMBARRASSED

Expansion
Contraction
Creative Energy
Destructive Energy

www.karakaraoguz.com

The way we perceive ourselves has A LOT to do with our energetic state and all that is put out to the Universe. This is a big reason why it is so important to do the inner work necessary so you can keep ascending to your highest self. The good vibes inspire health, happiness, optimism...this is a place we are able to heal and open our hearts, moving towards positive mental shifts. Remember: Mindset is everything!!!

In the good vibes, we can see new opportunities, are energized by our visions, are receptive to the energy that flows through us. We feel guided, supported and nourished by this flow of positive energy. Surround yourself with positive people. You are the company you keep...ya know? Birds of a feather flock together!!?!

IT IS SAID THAT YOU ARE THE AVERAGE OF YOUR 5 CLOSEST PEOPLE. SO WHO ARE YOU CHOOSING TO ASCEND TO YOUR HIGHEST SELF WITH?? THINK TO YOURSELF RIGHT NOW, WHO ARE YOUR PEOPLE AND EVALUATE THEIR ENERGETIC QUALITIES. ARE THEY MOVING FORWARD, BACKWARD, OR STANDING STILL IN LIFE? LIST YOUR 5 PEOPLE BELOW

I created the Emotional Vibrations Graphic on page 91. As you can see, emotions with lower energetic frequency are more constrictive and destructive in nature. Think about that for a minute. Think of

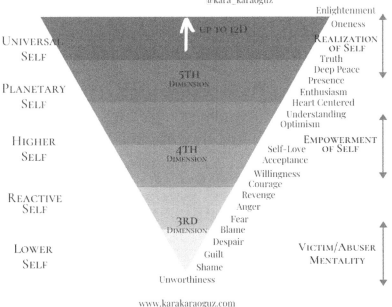

Spiritual Ascension Guide
Moving from 3D to 5D+ of Consciousness
@kara_karaoguz

UP TO 12D

UNIVERSAL SELF

PLANETARY SELF

HIGHER SELF

REACTIVE SELF

LOWER SELF

5TH DIMENSION

4TH DIMENSION

3RD DIMENSION

Enlightenment
Oneness
REALIZATION OF SELF
Truth
Deep Peace
Presence
Enthusiasm
Heart Centered
Understanding
Optimism

EMPOWERMENT OF SELF
Self-Love
Acceptance
Willingness
Courage
Revenge
Anger
Fear
Blame
Despair
Guilt
Shame
Unworthiness

VICTIM/ABUSER MENTALITY

www.karakaraoguz.com

how you feel in any of those emotional states and tune into how your body feels when you simply THINK of those states, let alone unpack and reside there! It's awful, right?? Alternatively, the higher energetic frequency states are expansive and creative in nature!! Yessss! Sign me up for those!! It is natural to move throughout all these emotions. We are human, after all. But remember that it's up to you to decide where you'd like to spend the majority of your time. You get to choose!

This second graphic is the Spiritual Ascension Guide, I love this graphic because I believe it accurately depicts the soul ascension process. And I LOVE the concept of Soul Ascension! As you can see, the lower vibrational states are more associated with the 3rd dimension of consciousness (3D) while mid level and higher vibrational states lead up to the 4th dimension (4D), the 5th dimension (5D) and beyond!! The goal of the soul's ascension is to move towards oneness and enlightenment AND to learn Unconditional Love. More on this in Chapter 11.

WHERE DO YOU SEE YOURSELF CURRENTLY SPENDING MOST OF YOUR TIME ON THIS SPIRITUAL ASCENSION GUIDE? WHERE DOES THE NEXT LEVEL VERSION OF YOU SPEND MOST OF HER TIME? WRITE ABOUT WHAT NEXT LEVEL YOU IS LIKE.

Lesson 7: Know Yourself

✦ It starts with you ✦

This is something I talk about a lot because it is essential to our growth and ascension!! You have to Love, Trust, Respect, Believe in, and Invest in your self first and foremost!!

This includes radical acceptance, positive self image, unconditional love of self! Loving YOURSELF is this is the greatest love of all!

When you love yourself fully, you experience inner stability and zero self-sabotage. Know that it is a journey, of dedication and devotion to value your imperfections and see only love. Look inside.

It is not uncommon for Empaths to get caught up in another person when coupled in a relationship. You may sometimes lose sight of who you are and what you enjoy. You may feel completely disconnected from yourself without even knowing it.

We have a tendency to look externally for validation, approval, acceptance. **If you rely on the external validation, that love will be ever ELUSIVE.** You will constantly be chasing it, begging for it, trying to convince others. And when you are so sure of the love you have for yourself, committed to a practice of turning inward and filling your own love tank, you will find fulfillment.

WHAT COMES TO MIND WHEN ASKED: **WHO ARE YOU?** WHAT TITLES DO YOU GIVE YOURSELF? WHAT ADJECTIVES DO YOU USE TO DESCRIBE YOURSELF? WHAT IS YOUR ESSENCE?

WHAT PARTS OF YOURSELF DO YOU OFTEN REJECT? INSECURITIES, SELF SABOTAGE, YOUR FEARS, CORE WOUNDS. THIS IS CALLED YOUR **SHADOW SELF**. WHAT COMES UP FOR YOU AROUND THIS CONCEPT?

What would life look and feel like if you radically accepted yourself and demonstrated unconditional self love?

Make a list of self-love activities you do now or want more of in life.

WHAT DO YOU REALLY WANT IN THIS LIFE?

HOW DO YOU WANT TO FEEL?

WHO DO YOU GET TO BE TO HAVE WHAT YOU WANT TO HAVE AND FEEL WHAT YOU WANT TO FEEL?

Lesson 8: Empaths

As you may or may not know, being an Empath means having diverse and dynamic sensitivities to others. We are sensing and picking up energy all day every day from every single person we come into contact with.

YOU ARE AN *Empath* IF...

@kara_karaoguz

1. You are able to sense the emotions of others
2. You can perceive the subtle changes in energy during conversations, shifts in dynamics, and possibly thoughts about things from others
3. You know when others are lying
4. You read body language like it's nobody's business
5. There is no such thing as casual sex
6. You feel your feelings intensely
7. You've been told "you're too sensitive", "toughen up", or been called a hypochondriac
8. You need alone time to recharge your batteries
9. Nature calls to you often and you find it very nurturing to spend time there
10. You don't enjoy small talk
11. You're intuitive AF
12. You get overwhelmed in large crowds
13. You are sensitive to sounds, smells, sights-really all your senses!
14. People confide in you
15. You tend to isolate

www.karakaraoguz.com

There are different types of Empaths, which can overlap and be present in the same individual:

Physical Empath: being in tune with what another is experiencing physically. This could be illness (medical empath) or, conversely, feeling a sense of joy and happiness, energized by being in their presence and their exuberance for life!! I love that feeling!

Emotional Empath: Holy sponge, Batman! When you are around others, you pick up their feelings and begin to take them on as you own. Ugh. Exhausting!!

Intuitive/Claircognizant Empath: sensing and picking up extraordinary sensations from another being: humans, animals, plants (plant empath), the Earth (geomantic), dreams, having premonitions, relationship/sexual empaths, and those even possessing the qualities of a medium, connecting to the other side of life.

I mentioned in Part I of this book that I realized I was an "Unaware" Empath when I was working in nursing. When I became aware of my

UNAWARE Empath

Feels exhausted and drained

Experiences co-dependent relationships

Often feels lost and confused

Not in touch with intuition or doubts self

Struggles with anxiety and low self esteem

Is a people pleaser at their own expense

Attracts narcissists and energy vampires

Experiences negative patterns and cycles of behavior

EMPOWERED Empath
@kara_karaoguz

Feels energized and aligned with purpose

Experiences secure, uplifting interdependent relationships

Is focused and confident

Deeply connected to and guided by intuition

Feels grounded, balanced, strong with healthy boundaries in place

May still attract narcs though deflects them and honors boundaries set

Is aware of tendency to repeat toxic cycles; that's enough to avoid them

A powerful manifestor; creates income doing what they love

situation, I was able to move towards becoming an "Empowered" Empath. I had to do this for my own sanity!! You can see in the previous graphic how these two types differ.

Lesson 9: Protective Practices for Empaths

Clean eating and drinking: You are taking on the energy of all you ingest, so....ingest wisely!!!

Morning grounding practices/routines that include meditation (see my Spiritual Guide for more)

Gems and crystals programmed for daily protection: Clear quartz, black onyx, black tourmaline, and selenite are some of my favorites for grounding and deflecting negative energies

Before leaving for the day, envision a glowing white gold swirling energy around you for protection and clearing, keep that shizzz swirling around you all day err day; it is powerful and protective

Head into nature as often as possible, especially when water is involved-waterfalls, beachfront, etc. This will restore and heal you to your very core!! It is ESSENTIAL.

Healthy Boundaries are a must. These are *Very Important* (more on boundaries in upcoming chapters)

Say Buh-Bye to the Energy Vamps......ya know, the ones who leave you high and dry after each interaction with them

Cleanse your space often with sage, palo Santo and essential oils, consider a waterfall protective practice or curtain shield

Rest, rest, and some more rest (when needed) to restore what has been depleted from you

Take baths often and allow yourself to luxuriate; throw a couple pounds of epsom salts in there, too

Release, have sex with someone you love, get moving: work out, lift weights, hike, do yoga, dance, etc

Journaling: Let your energy spill onto that paper, out of your body!! Then....onward! Don't dwell.

Every evening, cut the energetic cords between yourself and all those you encountered: With one hand out, palm up, and one hand on your heart, say: "Your energy back to you, my energy back to me"

Express Gratitude for this amazing gift

WHICH TYPE OF EMPATH DO YOU RESONATE MOST WITH?

WHAT HAVE YOU REGULARLY DONE TO PROTECT YOURSELF
ON A DAILY BASIS? WHAT ARE YOU MOST EXCITED TO
INCORPORATE?

Lesson 10: What is Love?

"*Love recognizes no barriers.*" -Maya Angelou

"*Love is friendship that has caught fire.*" -Ann Landers

"Love" is a noun **and** a verb! It's an intense feeling of deep affection, taking pleasure in something. Love is also feeling a deep romantic or sexual attachment to someone

Love is our essence. I love LOVE!! It's a complex set of emotions! Love is accepting oneself and another as is. Feeling an unwavering fondness, tenderness, devotion, passionate protectiveness and/or warmth towards oneself or another. Love is commitment, chemistry, compatibility with another. Love is unconditional! No expectations or limitations.

WRITE (IN DETAIL) ABOUT WHAT LOVE LOOKS AND FEELS LIKE TO YOU.

TAKE NOTE OF **WHERE** YOU FEEL THE SENSE OF **LOVE** IN YOUR PHYSICAL BODY. THIS IS SOMETHING THAT CAN CHANGE, DEPENDING ON CIRCUMSTANCE AND DIFFERENT DYNAMICS. JUST SIMPLY TUNE INTO THE FEELING AND LOCATION IN YOUR BODY NOW, IN THIS MOMENT.

WHAT ARE YOUR HOPES IN DIVING INTO THESE LESSONS WITHIN KEEP SHOWING UP? WHAT IS YOUR **INTENTION**?

Lesson 11: Mindfulness and Sensuality

Zen proverb: When walking, walk. When eating, eat.

Why mindfulness and sensuality? Because we have a physical body!!

"You don't have a soul, you are a soul. You have a body."

-C.S. Lewis

It is SO NECESSARY to get out of your head and INTO your body often. This is where the magic happens. You know how unproductive overthinking can be?? Yeah, me too. So focus on sensations in your body to help navigate during the hard times.

When I think about "sensuality," it has to do with our six senses... Perceiving the world around you through the SENSES!!!

Senses, sensual, sensuous...get it??!? The practice of being here now, conscious, mindful, aware, present.

Anyone has access to this, it just takes practice. This is YOUR body. You are safe in your body. You may need to remind yourself of this.

Keep your mind FULLY on what you're doing...taking it all in through the senses.

I'm most concerned with this quality of awareness that can be cultivated and practiced. Not moving from a place that's overly reactive and overwhelmed with life, more so responding to life around you. Remember: your ability to respond? This is a lifestyle! It is a continuous practice.

Practice perceiving the world through your senses. Any chance you get, think of it and practice being present and mindful as often as possible.

DROP INTO YOUR BODY NOW AND NOTICE WHAT YOU ARE EXPERIENCING VIA ALL SIX SENSES. WRITE ABOUT THAT.

Stay committed. Keep showing up, babes.

Lesson 12a: Love vs Fear

Plain and simple, Love > Fear!! I'm sure we've all found ourselves stuck in fear at one point in our lives! There are a million phenomenal quotes about love and fear...here are a couple I like.

"*Love is what we are born with, fear is what we learned here.*"

-Marianne Williamson

"There are two basic motivating forces: Fear and Love. When we are afraid, we pull back from life. When we are in love, we open to all that life has to offer with passion, excitement, and acceptance. We need to learn to love ourselves first, in all our glory and our imperfections. If we cannot love ourselves, we cannot fully open our ability to love others or our potential to create. Evolution and all hopes for a better world rest in the fearlessness and open-hearted vision of people who embrace life." -John Lennon

Don't forget: WE ARE ENERGETIC BEINGS!!!

Remember the graphic that depicts the vibrations of some common emotions we feel as humans. Take note!!

TWO BASIC FORCES IN LIFE

@kara_karaoguz

Love

- Reminds you of your gifts
- Speaks only the truth
- Encourages you to shine
- Peaceful and stable
- Builds
- Protects
- Has compassion for self and others
- Takes action
- Believes
- Heals
- High frequency
- Accepts and uplifts

Fear

- Focuses on flaws
- Tells lies
- Wants you to hide
- Defensive and impatient
- Destroys
- Attacks
- Compares self with others
- Makes excuses
- Doubts
- Wounds
- Low frequency
- Judges and critisizes

www.karakaraoguz.com

SIT WITH THESE TWO FORCES REFLECT ON HOW THEY APPLY TO YOUR LIFE. HOW DOES IT FEEL FOR YOU TO MOVE FROM FEAR?? HOW DOES IT FEEL TO MOVE FROM LOVE?

Lesson 12b: Kinds of LOVE

I had the pleasure of taking Greek and Roman mythology and art in college...I really enjoyed it!! And I love thinking of all the different states of love we can experience!! It's unrealistic to expect one person to fill all of our emotional needs!

The ancient Greeks identified seven different types of love:

Storage: natural affection, familial
Philia: friendship
Eros: romantic, sexual, erotic
Agape: unconditional, divine love
Ludus: flirting, playful, non-committed
Pragma: long-term, committed, married
Phalantia: self-love, self-esteem

FOR YOUR OWN REFLECTIONS, JOURNAL ABOUT EACH OF THESE TYPES OF LOVE AND SEE WHO FITS INTO THESE CATEGORIES IN YOUR LIFE?

Lesson 13: Intimacy

Intimacy is more than just sex. Sex is an important part of being intimate with someone but really for the most part, intimacy is so much more. **Honesty** is the highest form of intimacy. It's about being seen, heard, understood, feeling that there's a sense of familiarity, genuine connection. I always think of the word broken down by its' sounds: "Into Me See". See into Me. See Me.

 INTO-ME-SEE

Intimacy is being completely open, truthful, real, raw with someone who does not take any of it personally. Just full and complete acceptance and love. It has to be **reciprocal**. It has to go both ways in any relationship.

I talk a lot about safety and the importance of having it when you come from a trauma background. Healing happens when you are safe, when you are able to be stripped down to your naked soul and still be loved and accepted, held, cherished.

In order to feel intimate with someone else we must <u>first be intimate with ourselves</u>. That's how we know what allows us to open to another and be vulnerable, and to know what is a detriment, what leads us to close ourselves off. The goal in relationships is to have others really know us.

We started off this work exploring what "love" means to you. In the previous pages, you've had a chance for reflections to ponder and dig deeper into who you are and what your beliefs are about different topics contained so far in this book.

Also remember it is natural to learn new things about yourself when in relationship with another. You don't need to have it all figured out before getting into a relationship. There are many parts of ourselves we don't know, that we're unfamiliar with. And that's okay!

What is very interesting about heterosexual relationships is the concept of touch points. According to one theory, men only need one touch point to stimulate arousal and create a desire for sex while women need an average of 22! These touch points include anything that is visual, auditory, emotional, sensory, etc.

So if you are coupled in a heterosexual relationship, remember the importance of creating the touch points in an equal shared sense!

WHAT DO YOU DO THAT ALLOWS YOUR SIGNIFICANT OTHER TO
UNDERSTAND YOU BETTER?

WHAT DO YOU DO THAT DISCONNECTS YOU FROM ALLOWING
YOUR PARTNER TO UNDERSTAND YOU BETTER?

IN THINKING ABOUT THE TOUCH POINTS, ANSWER THE
FOLLOWING STATEMENTS AND THINK IN TERMS OF
EMOTIONAL WELLBEING AND CONNECTION, INTELLECTUAL
DESIRES, YOUR HOME OR THE ENVIRONMENT YOU CHOOSE TO
BE IN, PHYSICAL CONTACT OR SEX.

When I receive_____(xyz connection, emotional for example),
I feel intimately connected to my partner because

_____.

Continue writing out these types of statements, thinking of as many
touch points and avenues of receiving love/intimacy as possible.

CHAPTER 8

Taking It Back

"I'm not what happened to me, I am what I choose to become." -Carl Jung

We're taking it back...waaaaaayyyyyyy back. To your upbringing!! Because all that is effecting your current day Adult relationships now. I can not stress that enough!!!

Lesson 14: Family of Origin

"Family of Origin" (FOO) refers to your significant caretakers and siblings you grew up with. These are the family dynamics that you were born or adopted into.

And Hoooo-leeee shiiit does this all play into who you are today! Those dynamics affect every aspect of your life now. The purpose here is to raise awareness and make connections with how you're showing up in present day.

The family of origin stuff could be having a positive or negative affect on you depending on the dynamics.

List the positive (+) and negative (-) qualities, characteristics, traits of each person that comes to mind within your FOO. See page 119 for help with adjectives.

NAME:

+   -

NAME:

+   -

NAME:

+   -

NAME:

+   -

NAME:

+   -

List of Adjectives

active	daring	independent	responsible
adventurous	dependable	insistent	restless
affectionate	determined	intelligent	rowdy
afraid	dishonest	jealous	rude
ambitious	disrespectful	jovial	sarcastic
anxious	dreamer	lazy	secretive
argumentative	eager	leader	self-confident
attentive	easy-going	logical	selfish
bewildered	efficient	lonely	self-reliant
bossy	energetic	lovable	sensitive
brave	enthusiastic	loving	shy
brilliant	fair	loyal	silly
bully	faithful	lucky	sincere
calm	fidgety	mature	skillful
capable	fierce	mean	sly
careful	foolish	moody	smart
caring	friendly	mysterious	sneaky
charismatic	funny	nervous	snobbish
charming	generous	noisy	sociable
childish	gentle	obedient	stingy
clever	gloomy	obnoxious	strict
clumsy	greedy	observant	stubborn
cold-hearted	grouchy	optimistic	studious
compassionate	hard-working	peaceful	sweet
competitive	happy	persistent	talented
conceited	harsh	pessimistic	talkative
concerned	hateful	picky	thoughtful
confident	hopeful	pleasant	thoughtless
conscientious	hopeless	polite	timid trusting
considerate	humorous	proud	trustworthy
cooperative	ignorant	puzzled	unfriendly
courageous	imaginative	quick	useful versatile
cowardly	immature	quiet	warm-hearted
critical	impatient	reliable	wise witty
cruel	impolite	respectful	worried
curious	impulsive		

WHAT STANDS OUT TO YOU ABOUT CREATING THOSE LISTS?
HOW HAS THIS INFLUENCED YOUR VIEW OF LOVE?

WHAT ARE THE TOP 3 TRAITS YOU WANT TO TAKE WITH YOU
TO YOUR ROMANTIC AND LOVING RELATIONSHIPS?

WHAT ARE THE TOP 3 TRAITS YOU DON'T WANT TO TAKE
WITH YOU TO YOUR RELATIONSHIPS?

IN YOUR UPBRINGING, WHAT DID THE PRESENCE OF LOVE FEEL LIKE? WHAT DID THE ABSENCE OF LOVE FEEL LIKE?

WAS THERE ANYTHING YOU WANTED AS A CHILD THAT YOU DIDN'T GET?

IS THERE ANYTHING YOU WISH YOUR FOO DID DIFFERENTLY? DO YOU WISH YOUR FOO NOTICED A CERTAIN SOMETHING ABOUT YOU?

HOW WERE DISCIPLINED AS A CHILD?

DESCRIBE YOURSELF AS A CHILD.

Lesson 15: Inner Child Work

To say that anyone made it out of childhood unscathed would be a complete fallacy!! Everyone has something. It is said that 70% of people have experienced trauma in their lives; I feel like its more than that! Now after the COVID_19 pandemic, every single person has lived through something traumatic.

The "inner child" is the unconscious part of our mind where we've packed away unmet needs, suppressed child-like emotions, stuffed down our intuition, our creativity, and our playful nature.

Without getting tooo in depth with this technique, sit quietly in meditation and be open to **receiving an age in your life that needs healing**. If you recall a painful event or trauma, start there then connect with the child in you at that age. Give this child everything she needed at the time of the painful event/trauma. Validate her. Accept her. See her, hold her, protect her, love her unconditionally, guide her, nurture her, respect her, choose her, tell her she belongs, whatever she needs. Understand that she is YOU. Know that you are safe, protected, loved, and guided now, as an adult. Be the adult the child you needed.

Until this version of yourself is healed, we continue to view the world through this wounded lens. Those who need healing in this area may act out in the same way as a child: yelling and screaming, stomping around, slamming doors or shutting down/giving the silent treatment. You may get defensive very easily or completely deny someone else's experience all together.

Connect to your younger self by coloring, watching a kids movie, taking a bubble bath, having a stuffed animal! I have also created a photo collage and typed in statements and questions I am saying or conveying to my inner child. This technique has worked for my clients too.

Let your inner child sit right next to you when you're getting work done, bring her to run errands or on your fun adventures.

You can also write your inner child a love note. You can do this for any age or multiple ages...but for the sake of starting out, choose one age that stands out the most. Intuitively trust that that's the age that needs the most attention in order for your healing and ascension to be optimized now. I created this graphic for myself, with my Nini.

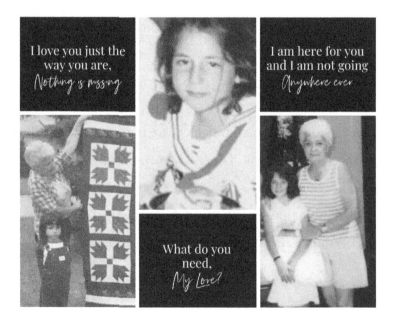

Lesson 16: Reparenting

Reparenting is showing up for yourself now as your adult self for your adult self.

There are many things we can do to work with reparenting. In order to bring in more stability for yourself welcome in consistent action. Consistent sleep, eating, daily exercise and movement. It is necessary to shift inner dialogue; be the voice of a loving parent. Set and honor healthy boundaries, follow through on your word to self, believe in yourself, know your worth, shed codependent tendencies, give up unhealthy coping mechanism like drinking to excess or smoking, meet your own core needs of being seen, heard, loved on all levels of your being.

There are activities you can do to maintain and heal this area of life: meditations, more writing, lists, connections. For the sake of this book, let's keep it relatively simple and write a love letter to yourself. Also, put some "rules" in place to practice giving yourself more structure. Reparenting the shit out of yourself on your path to wholeness!!

Lesson 17: Five Stages of Grief (The Kubler Ross model)

Whenever you are processing a loss of any kind: death of a loved one, death of a relationship, death of a former version of yourself, you will inevitably move through your own stages of grieving. This model I am referring to here was first introduced by a Swiss Psychiatrist named Elisabeth Kubler-Ross in her book *On Death and Dying* (1969).

Semi-Side Note: Know that experiencing a "Lone Wolf" phase, as I call it, during this process is entirely appropriate. As you grow and change, expect old friends to fall off and new friends (who are more aligned with your Next Level) to start filtering in. When you commit to a healthier lifestyle, releasing old patterns and circumstances, peeps who knew the old you may push back. Let them. This is your path. Keep moving forward with your growth and evolution. There may be a lull between the *old friends* and the *new friends*. You may feel sad or antsy. This is a great time to get to know yourself better. To love yourself and show up for yourself in ways you are wanting others to for you. This is part of your healing journey.

"We are all just walking each other home." -Ram Dass

Okay, back to the stages...

The five stages of grief are: Denial, Anger, Bargaining, Depression, and Acceptance.

In **Denial**, we may be avoidant. We may feel confusion, shock, fear, and a lot of uncertainty. There is a sense of overwhelm and complete disbelief. This process of denial helps us during the grieving process because it allows for an integration of this new information. It sort of gives us more time to wrap our heads around the news.

In **Anger**, we may feel intense irritation, rage, anxiety or frustration. Often times it is a really fun mix of all those emotions. We may want to blame others or wonder "why is this happening to me?!". I often say that anger is sad's body guard, protecting us from all the hurt and pain that is hidden beneath the surface. In this situation, anger serves a valuable purpose. It can be very energizing when channeled appropriately. It helps give us strength to keep moving forward because...time marches on and the clock stops for no one.

Next we come to **Bargaining**. Lordy Lordy, I seemed to have been stuck in this phase for a VERY long time. As a "hopeless romantic" and an eternal optimist, I focus on the good in people and situations, as I've mentioned before. Because of this I feel I end up dragging myself through the dirt for far longer than someone who does not view the world like I do.

Bargaining is when we are struggling to find meaning in the situation. We wish and hope and pray so hard that if only this would be this way then that would be that way. If only, if only, if only...all the what ifs. The hope is that maybe we could avoid the grief through some type of negotiation. As unsettling as this realization was, it is necessary to see it: it is false hope.

Then moving onto **Depression**, we may feel helpless, numb, exhausted, a desire to leave the situation altogether, little to no motivation to do anything. It's a sad time. The anger has slipped away, revealing the deep sorrow you feel in your heart. This isn't how your life was "supposed to be". This wasn't the plan. There is an emptiness, a hollow, a void in the depths of your soul. Life as you knew it no longer exists. We may isolate, withdraw, not reach out to others for support though this is a time in the grieving process when we really need the love, support and guidance of others.

And finally, gloriously moving to **Acceptance**. Hallelujah! This is the final stage of grief in the Kubler-Ross model. We start to explore new options in life, putting new plans in place and move on. That's not to say there isn't still sadness but we keep showing up and continue to move forward with the healing journey. The good days tend to outweigh the bad days. During this time, the emotions begin to stabilize and we make peace with all that has transpired. We release the fantasy of what we thought our life or our relationship was going to be. We see that "Ideal vs Real" are two totally different realities. The truth hurts but here, we're more able to see it. We wrap our heads around the fact that we can't change the way the wind blows but we can learn to redirect our sails. Redirect those sails, My Love. Keep growing, evolving, expanding into your new normal.

It is also worth mentioning: you HAVE to have moved through the **Acceptance** phase of grief before any of these next practices in forgiveness will be effective.

FUNDAMENTAL TRUTH

a kara_karaoguz

"YOU LOOK AT THE TREE AND YOU ALLOW IT. I PRACTICE TURNING PEOPLE INTO TREES, WHICH MEANS *Appreciating them just as they are.*"

RAM DASS

www.karakaraoguz.com

The way the Kubler-Ross Model presents is linear. Based on my personal experience and from what I have seen with my coaching clients, it is entirely possible to move in and out of these states fluidly. Typically, once you get to the later 2 stages, you will continue to move forward with your healing, processing and integrating. To me, healing from trauma and unhealthy relationships reminds me of a spiral, we keep circling back and circling back, each time gaining more awareness and insight to ultimately make a decision for yourself that is most aligned with your vision for your future. Recovery, learning effective coping strategies, and moving towards wholeness are all available to you. Reach out if you are needing support.

Lesson 18a: Forgiveness and Making Peace

This is something we, as a society, don't really talk about. We've all heard that holding onto anger or grudges is like drinking poison and expecting it to kill the other person. We know we need to forgive, though the actual action gets brushed over with phrases like "just let it go" or "Don't worry about that", etc. Other words synonymous for forgive are pardon, overlook, excuse, ignore, understanding.

So HOWWWWWWWW?? How do we find forGIVEness?? HOWWW do we make peace with that which caused us harm??

Lots of ways! You can try them all or pick and choose. You will make this practice your OWN!

Please remember that the process of forgiveness is ongoing. It's like a spiral. You'll revisit the same traumas over and over, freeing yourself from the entrapment you may feel when replaying your old narratives.

After you have moved through the 5-point process of Finding ForGIVEness shared here, cleanse your space w sage, Palo Santo, or essential oils, take a warm soothing epsom salt bath, drink lots of water and be good to yourself. Self love is one way to take back your power.

In order to advance to the next level in life and in business, we must forgive to make space for new!!

If we are holding onto the low vibe feelings/shitty energy (e.g.: negative feelings, hurt, trauma, betrayals, etc) then we are STUCK and no matter how much you want to move forward, it won't happen. When we forGIVE and genuinely release "it", we remove the resentment and are free to ascend towards our highest self, ready to receive all we are actively calling in with our New Moon Intentions and any other manifestation practices you may have.

Lesson 18b: 5-Point Process of ForGIVEness

The 5-Point Process of Forgiveness consists of: Awareness, Acknowledge, Replace, Reframe, Release. Do The Work and apply this technique to what you feel you're ready to forgive.

AWARENESS: ALL OF THE BELIEFS UNDERNEATH YOUR ACTIONS. BECOME AWARE OF WHAT NEEDS TO BE RELEASED FROM THE SAD TIMES.

ACKNOWLEDGE: CHILDHOOD MEMORIES, EXPERIENCES, SCRIPTS HANDED DOWN FROM GENERATION TO GENERATION, SHAME, UNJUST RESPONSIBILITY, BLAME, ANGER, ALL THAT HAS MADE YOU FEEL SMALL, LESS THAN OR INFERIOR. WHAT DO YOU GET TO ACKNOWLEDGE ABOUT THE PRESSING ISSUE?

REPLACE: WITH POSITIVE THOUGHTS, MANTRA, AFFIRMATION TO STATE EVERY TIME THESE BLOCKS COME UP (GIVE MY EXAMPLE THAT STRONG SAFE MEN SURROUND PROTECT ME OFFERING THE RESPECT AND INTEGRITY AT ALL TIMES), THE GOAL IS PEACE AND FEELINGS OF FREEDOM-SERENITY. YOU DESERVE PEACE.

REFRAME: FIND THE SILVER LINING TO EACH SHITTY EXPERIENCE. STATE "I AM SO GLAD _____ HAPPENED BECAUSE _____."

RELEASE-FREEDOM FROM THE FEELINGS, FEEL INTO PEACE CALM, HARMONY, RELIEF. AS PREVIOUSLY MENTIONED, THE FULL MOON IS A GREAT TIME ENERGETICALLY TO RELEASE THE STUFF. YOU CAN LIST THE THINGS AND THEN TAKE THAT LIST SHRED, TEAR, CRINKLE IT UP, OR BURN IT OR ALL OF

**THE ABOVE AS YOUR REPROGRAMMING YOUR NEW THOUGHT
PATTERNS!!**

Additional Fun Practices that serve as means to take back your power
if you have been an "Unaware" Empath:

Lesson 18c: Ho'oponoopono

Sometimes referred to as a mantra or prayer, this shamanic
technique in interpreted as "to make (doubly) right".

It's a practice of energetic healing, emotional cleansing and spiritual
clearing to reconcile all that is not in alignment with who we are. To
keep the explanation simple, it is all about helping the subconscious
mind take responsibility for our perception and experience of things.
Ho'oponopono only requires one person and all that is needed is
your presence.

This Hawaiian forgiveness technique can be practiced in two ways:

1. With thoughts of one person in particular who has caused you
   pain. Through the practice, you are reaching out on a soul level.
2. By creating an entire list of all the instances, situations, trauma,
   people, etc that that have harmed you and you are needing to
   reconcile and make peace with then addressing them each
   individually.

The technique consists of the chant or repetition of 4 key phrases:

Thank You
I'm sorry
I forgive you
I love you

Regardless of whether you are addressing one or many, allow yourself to get grounded and bring yourself in the moment. This can all be done in your mind or on paper.

Thank you for the lessons...and, gratitude. I'm sorry for xyz to myself and to you. I forgive you (to yourself and the other person). I love you (to yourself and the other person). Remember, all is mirrored back to you. If you're using the technique w one person in mind (option 1), bring to mind a person/situation that has harmed you and you are needing to Reconcile and make peace with. Repeat the mantra to that person: Thank You, I'm sorry, I forgive you, I love you.

If you're creating an entire list of all the situations and trauma that you are holding on to and are ready to let go of then I suggest you follow suit with format below. On each line, write out what ails you and keep going, filling the lines, until you can't think of any more. Then go back and review the list, reading each of your statements followed by the mantra of the Ho'oponopono. Let yourself feel into it. Be aware of any sensations that come up on all levels-physically, emotionally, mentally, spiritually and just allow yourself to observe without judgment.

THANK YOU. I'M SORRY. I FORGIVE YOU. I LOVE YOU

THANK YOU. I'M SORRY. I FORGIVE YOU. I LOVE YOU

THANK YOU. I'M SORRY. I FORGIVE YOU. I LOVE YOU

THANK YOU. I'M SORRY. I FORGIVE YOU. I LOVE YOU

THANK YOU. I'M SORRY. I FORGIVE YOU. I LOVE YOU

Lesson 18d: Energetic Cord Cutting

DO THE WORK

@kara_karaoguz

ENERGETIC CORD CUTTING

WHAT IS IT? AND

...How To...

www.karakaraoguz.com

**Energetic cord cutting
AKA Etheric Cords
Psychic Energy Cords
Emotional Attachments**

These are the connections; the energy structures

formed when in relationship with all those we choose to engage with. The etheric cords service channels of communication in our subtle body.

This practice involves clearing the energetic cords and connections you may feel towards instances, situations, trauma, people, etc. A cord is created when you have an emotional experience w someone or something in your life.

We inevitably have unspoken, karmic attachments to others when emotional pain has been caused or inflicted. It is very important to release the energy and cut the cord(s) that are tied to pain, trauma, guilt, resentment in order to raise your frequency as you ascend to a new level of your being.

When you reach a point in your own progression that this connection is:
✖ depleting your energy
✖ creating an energy leak
✖ you realize the relationship is toxic
✖ you see aspects of the attachment are dark, non-productive, small, insecure, etc. it's time to sever the cord

Release the negative cords of attachment! In doing so, you were declaring your energetic boundaries.

There is no right or wrong way to do this. You may find yourself visualizing this practice as many times as necessary until you achieve the desired results.

Get still

Sit quietly and call on your angels and spirit guides to be with you

Take deep breaths in and let them out slowwww

Feel into your body

Envision the cord as silver, glowing, any color of your choice, the thickness of your choice (representative of the relationship)

See this cord connecting you and the other person you wish to be free from. Become aware of where in your body you feel the cord attached to.

Thank them for the lessons.

See yourself safely holding a large pair of shears, scissors ✂ , a sword ⚔ , and axe 🪓 (!!!!)...you get to choose-make this practice your own!

Begin cutting the cord while thinking or saying out loud phrases like

✔ "only positive, affirming, supportive connections"

✔ "release me from this toxic bond"

✔ "with deep love and grace, my energy back to me, your energy back to you"

✔ "only love and light"

Envision a white light that surrounds you, cleansing your aura and your energetic field. Feeling at peace with a renewed sense of self. You are whole and complete.

This is a very empowering exercise.

When the connection is healthy the energy is calming, pleasant and up-lifting.

Ideally the cord of connection is heart to heart insecure. Unhealthy energetic cords me connect to the solar plexus or sacral chakra's, signifying control or sexual manipulation. Be aware of these and move forward.

Use this visualization to remove and cut all energetic cords not aligned with your greater good.

Honor your highest self. Cutting energetic cords is necessary to advance to your next level, embodying your highest purpose.

We are energetic beings! It's necessary to prune your energetic cords from time to time.

The negative energy can only be dissolved or converted to positive energy. This is done through forgiveness and love. Forgiveness heals the trauma.

Lesson 18e: EFT

This is an acronym for Emotional Freedom Technique and is also referred to as Tapping. It is a form of psychological acupressure and is often utilized with counseling to heal trauma and invoke forgiveness in addition to acupuncture, NLP (neuro-linguistic programming), and energy medicine. This technique serves to clear disturbances in your energetic pathways. The tapping releases the disturbances.

There are ten points (14 total though some intersect so we focus on ten). There is a process to performing this technique. Prior to moving systematically through the points 3x, you intentionally focus on a painful emotion or situation. You then rate how you feel 0-10, 10 being the most emotional intensity. You create a "reminder phrase" explaining what is ailing you. It goes something like this:

"Even though I am <u>really fucking pissed off about so & so</u>, I deeply and profoundly love and accept myself."

You fill in the blank for your reminder phrase. Then move through the points, stating the phrase with each new point, staying with the emotion. After two passes, take a deep breath and reassess the emotional intensity based on the 0-10 scale. Ideally, each time you re-assess, the intensity drops by two point markers.

This is an effective technique to incorporate into your healing toolkit. I have used it many times and it works!

Lesson 18f: Shower/Energetic Cleansing

This is a fun, simple practice. When you shower imagine all your anxieties, worries, stressors being rinsed from your body, mind and soul and going down the drain, never to be part of you again. Likewise if you take a soothing epsom salts bath, soak all the stressors out and then when you open the drain and the water is leaving the basin, so are your worries. Through this practice you make peace and find forgiveness for all that is troubling you.

Lesson 18g: Timeline/Storytelling

This is the practice of creating a healing timeline. Take out a sheet of paper or your beloved journal. Create a timeline of your life and write down any and all important life events.

You can list it in a vertical or horizontal format. Some options of events to list are:

• Births
• Deaths
• Graduations
• Marriages
• Divorces
• Job transitions
• Moves
• Vacations
• Surgeries +/or hospitalizations
• Major illnesses

What to do with this info??

Become aware of any shifts or changes you experienced in life. Sometimes, when we have a better understanding of the Why, we are able to find peace and healing.

This is a project in increasing self-awareness. If an event is standing out more than others, you have a better idea of what you need to address and heal in order to forgive and continue progressing forward to your next level.

Lesson 18h: Declutter

How much stuff do you have around your home that's just taking up space?? All of those occupy your energetic field and can feel draining. Make time to declutter. To free up space so you can welcome in anew!!

Some places you can reorganize:

Delete old apps
Clear inbox of emails
Empty junk drawer
Organize closet (keep, donate, toss)
Update calendars
Clean desk area
Your purse
Your home: garage, entryway, basement, closets, bedroom, etc
Clear mind with meditation
After you declutter, be sure to cleanse with sage, instilling new vibration and reprogramming new frequency

Lesson 18i: Bach Original Flower Remedies

This was one of the first energy healing modalities I got certified in because I experienced such amazing results with the Rescue Remedy (RR). As mentioned in Part I, when my panic attacks were in full swing, RR helped me through them.

The 38 flower essences are used to treat emotional imbalances so you can enjoy better physical health. It's clear that our state of mind affects our ability to heal from an illness or our general overall health and happiness. With health and happiness comes peace of mind and a greater sense of enjoying life. When we're not stressed out all the time we can direct our energy and attention to other things. We know this!

Dr. Edward Bach was a physician in England in the early 1900s. He developed this simple system of healing so it could be accessible to everyone and ultimately we'd be able to heal ourselves. #IntuitiveSelfHealers!!

He grouped the 38 essences into seven different categories:
• Fear
• Uncertainty
• Insufficient interest in the present moment
• Loneliness
• Over-sensitivity to the influence of others
• Despondency and despair
• Over-care for the welfare of others

These categories help you narrow down exactly what imbalance you're feeling in greater detail.

So if you're feeling fear, what kind of fear? Or if you're feeling despair, what kind of despair?

These essences are all natural and safe for all with no side effects or interactions. They're extremely compatible with other therapies. It takes a certain amount of honesty and self-awareness to be able to identify your feelings.

These flower essences have supported me through major life transitions many times!! It's for real. I so believe in them!!

The tinctures are taken orally, usually dropped into water and consumed. Ya know how you can't swim during a thunder and lightning storm (I love thunderstorms!!)?? Same principle. The water carries the healing energy of the flower. It's best to narrow down the primary issues then combine up to 6-7 at a time in a glass of water and drink. Or they can be made into little dropper bottle "potions," as I like to call them! That way, the same combination can be administered to help squash the emotional imbalances thoroughly over a period of three weeks when taken consistently (recommended dose: two drops 4x/day until the potion is gone).

Lesson 18j: Discharging and Transmuting Energy through Movement

This is vital.

Move. Every. Single. Day.

Remember in Part I, I mentioned all the tears I cried during my yoga practices? As my body was safely releasing the sadness, tension, trauma? That's this.

Imagine not ever incorporating any movement into your days... you'll feel lousy.

Stagnant energy in your physical body is a no-go during emotional healing. You can discharge the negative emotions and energy by stomping, marching, running, yoga, boxing, lifting weights, or one of my favorites: really hard 20-pound ball slams.

However you choose to move, trust that it will be therapeutic and healing. Gotta keep the energy flowing.

Lesson 18k: Full Moon Release

I love to follow the moon phases. I founded my birth business, New Moon Healing, in 2010. I chose the name because new moons are symbolic of new beginnings! And birthing a baby is one hell of a new beginning!! Also because I love the concept of manifestation. More on that in upcoming chapters.

The Full Moon is a time to let go of what is not serving you. To release all that no longer aligns with your vision of life. So first and foremost, you have to be aware of what that vision is. That's why we do the work to get clear on who you are and what you want. Then each month, on the full moon, you get to perform a ritual to shed the "shit" from you and work towards forgiveness.

In my Spiritual Guide to Living with Intention I detail this practice. I also typically post the reminders on my social media pages as well as email those on my list so, if you're interested in those reminders, join me!

CHAPTER 9

The Game Changers

"We delight in the beauty of the butterfly and rarely admit the changes it has gone through to achieve that beauty."

-Maya Angelou

Lesson 19: Polyvagal Theory

The Polyvagal Theory was created in the mid 1990s by Stephen Porges, a neonatologist who first studied how the birth experience impacted the early days of a baby's life. I'm all about that too!

He had no idea what an impact this theory would have on individuals healing from trauma. The Polyvagal Theory affects individuals by giving them an understanding of the neurophysiological explanations for behavior after we have lived through trauma. It's genius!! For those of us with a history of trauma, this theory helps us view our responses through the lens of compassion so that healing can ensue. Let's be honest, we sometimes have the tendency to be hard on ourselves and overly critical. Learning about this theory allows us to soften this view of self.

In recent years, this amazing theory has been applied to therapy and work in adult relationship dynamics. I have a class devoted to this topic for sale on my website: www.karakaraoguz.com.

It is said that "story follows form" because our Autonomic Nervous System (ANS) reacts BEFORE our thoughts or emotions. Only after the chemical messengers are coursing through our veins does emotion get hooked to the situation and then thoughts. See how "story follows form" is at play?

Because I love to teach and talk about natural, physiological birth, I have been teaching about the nervous system to my birth doula clients for a decade. Our ANS responds to threats (real or perceived). We have something called "neuroception" that refers to this task of constantly scanning for threats and evaluating risks. It is a beautiful system that allows for our survival!! In my years being sexually abused and then later raped, my nervous system made me immobile (dorsal vagal activation) to keep me ALIVE! It really is amazing.

THIS IS HUGE SO PLEASE TAKE NOTE!!!!

While I very deeply believe in moving towards 5D awareness and consciousness, the reality is that we are here in this physical body. Our soul, hanging out in this body, for this lifetime. With that being the case, I hold firm that it's important to understand what our chemical messengers are doing, unbeknownst to us, and how we can work together to create more harmony.

Ahead of our thoughts, mindset, feelings, emotions we have our PHYSIOLOGY that fires off. These are our hormones and chemical messengers. They communicate in all different ways and affect all of our organs and the systems of our bodies.

Being a nurse and birth professional, I totally dig this nerdy stuff!! And being able to apply it to healing from trauma and *show up* in the context of LOVE more fully, I can really get down with that!!

Anyways, when in conflict or confronted with threat (real or perceived) we respond in one of four ways: F/F/F/F!!! We go into Fight, Flight, Freeze, or Fawn.

We're mostly familiar with these responses. Fight refers to the physical act of fighting off a threat or the verbal act in the form of harsh words. Flight is feeling the need to GTFO and leave the situation. Fawn is a newer concept within this structure. Fawning is smoothing things over after a conflict without any real resolution or repair. When one does this, it's often at one's own expense. I used to fawn. And then we have Freeze aka complete shutdown.

Knowing how you typically respond is ESSENTIAL to understanding yourself better. When you identify how you show up for yourself and for others you can start having compassion and an increase in sense of self love.

Something worth mentioning is that these responses we have are ALL designed for our survival. They are all meant to keep us safe in some way. Understanding this is key to healing. Our system is working its hardest to keep you alive and thriving! Thanks evolution! For one reason or another, you move into F/F/F/F. We are meant to move up and down the ANS ladder throughout the day as our body beautifully responds to threats.

There are ways to unlearn and relearn more appropriate, useful ways to regulate your own physiology and nervous system.

The gist of the theory is that there are three physiological states we experience. At the top of the ANS ladder, you see the Ventral Vagal Activation. When we are in this state, we feel safe and are able to engage socially with others. We feel at ease and are completely free to be ourselves. When in the Ventral Vagal state, we are curious and open to new possibilities. We're calm and at peace. We're present and grounded in who we are and likely to experience more joy.

THE 4 F'S
ANS RESPONSES TO THREATS
@kara_karaoguz

FIGHT	FAWN
Actions: Mobilized, Panicked	Actions: Mobilized, Freaking out
Physically: Increased HR, breathing, pupils dilated, perspiration, tense, upright posture, skin is flushed	Physically: Increased HR, breathing, pupils dilated, Antsy, Graspy
Emotions: Anxious, Fearful, Frustrated, Rage, Anger, tendency to blame, insult, be cruel, confronting	Emotions: Intense need to smooth things over, obsessive thoughts, racing emotions, feeling "on edge", go along with whatever is threatening
Actions: Run away, Irritation	Actions: Immobilized, Shut down
Physically: Increased HR, breathing, pupils dilated, digestion slows, pale skin, may be trembling or shaking	Physically: Eyes may look spaced out or fixed, may feel nauseous or even vomit, flat facial expression, collapsed body language, slower breathing, may go to sleep
Emotions: Wants "it" to stop, leaves situation, seeks safety, avoidance, denial, wants to escape, doesn't want to talk or rehash situation	Emotions: limited thoughts about situation, blank, numb, disconnected, unable to process information
FLIGHT	FREEZE

www.karakaraoguz.com

When a threat (real or perceived) enters the scene, perceived via neuroception, the ANS goes into Sympathetic Activation. You know this state. This state has you feeling panicked and mobilized... you need to MOVE! You're fearful, anxious, irritated, frustrated, graspy, on edge. Your thoughts are racing, you're "on edge," you want to escape or you feel an intense need to smooth things over. All in attempts to get you back to the Ventral Vagal state. In order to get back up the ladder, you have to get your shit together! You are the only one coming to your rescue here. The task when you're in this state is to self-regulate! Self-regulation consists of anything that will help calm you down. The journal prompts that follow give you a chance to start your list of "glimmers," the activities that give you a glimmer of hope that you can stop freaking out.

Then, in more extreme cases of neuroception when the threat feels inescapable, you move into Dorsal Vagal Activation. This state is major collapse, shutdown, immobilization. You may feel numb, dissociated, disconnected, hopeless, helpless, spaced out, unable to process any information. You may also feel trapped or intense shame. In order to get yourself up and out of this state, you GET TO get moving. Mobilize. Walk. Pace. Just move!! The task or assignment is to co-regulate which means get your shit together WITH someone else too. So walking together, talking, breathing together, lying together until you come up the ladder, moving through the anxiety and other associated emotions of the Sympathetic Activation then happily onto the Ventral Vagal State!

When one has a history of trauma or abuse, you may get "stuck" in the sympathetic or dorsal activations. Learning as much about yourself and how you respond to threats is your ticket to freedom. The goal is peace, stability and more of an even-keeled existence. Amiright?? Learning about Regulation (self- or co-regulation) is money! That's your gold.

AUTONOMIC *Nervous System* LADDER
a kara_karaoguz
BASED ON THE POLYVAGAL THEORY

ENGAGED

SAFE
SOCIAL

MOBILIZED
PANICKED

FIGHT
FLIGHT
FAWN

IMMOBLIZE
SHUTDOWN

FREEZE
COLLAPSE

MOVE UP AND DOWN LADDER WITH EASE AND FLEXIBILITY BASED ON STATE OF AROUSAL

VENTRAL VAGAL ACTIVATION
Feeling at ease, free to really be yourself
Open to new possibilities
Calm, PeaceFULL
Present, Grounded
Curious
Mindful, Joyful

SYMPATHETIC ACTIVATION
Fearful, Anxious, Worried
Rage, Irritation, Frustration
Racing, obsessive thoughts
Feeling "on edge", wanting to escape
Intense need to smooth things over even though
no resoultion

DORSAL VAGAL ACTIVATION
Numb, Disconnected, Hopeless
Helpless, Depressed
Spaced out, unable to process information accurately
Intense Shame, Feel Trapped

www.karakaraoguz.com

TASK: SELF REGULATION

TASK: CO-REGULATION

I place a lot of importance on **Stress Resilience**, as opposed to stress reduction!! There will inevitably be stressors in our lives, we will feel threatened, we will be triggered in relationships. It's a fact of life.

Having a flexible nervous system and resilient vagal tone is the goal. Trauma creates an inflexible nervous system so we have to consciously, purposefully reprogram!!

WHERE DO YOU SEE YOURSELF SPENDING MOST OF YOUR TIME ON THE AUTONOMIC LADDER (REFER TO GRAPHIC ON PAGE 152)? ON A DAY TO DAY BASIS AS WELL AS DURING CONFLICT?

WHAT *TASK* (RIGHT SIDE OF ANS LADDER GRAPHIC) DO YOU FEEL IS MOST BENEFICIAL TO YOUR REGULATION?

Let's talk "Triggers and Glimmers." Deb Dana, author of *The Polyvagal Theory in Therapy,* has coined these terms. Start here in creating your lists.

TRIGGERS: THE THINGS THAT SET YOU OFF, WHEN YOU FEEL THREATENED

GLIMMERS: ACTIVITIES THAT GIVE YOU A GLIMMER OF HOPE FOR GETTING BACK TO THE SAFETY OF THE VENTRAL VAGAL STATE. FOR ME, I PET KODA OR HAVE SOME MOVEMENT WITH HIM (WALK, RUN, HIKE), GET ON MY MAT AND PRACTICE YOGA, JOURNAL OR WRITE, LISTEN TO MUSIC, DANCE, LIGHT MY INCENSE, GET ESSENTIAL OILS GOING, COOK, CLEAN, ETC.

THE IMPORTANCE OF REGULATION. CAN YOU SEE HOW LEARNING REGULATION SKILLS WILL BENEFIT YOU MOVING FORWARD?

Lesson 20: Yoga and Somatic Experiencing

It is of the UTMOST importance, move your body daily! Embody your vision of being free of anxiety, uncertainty, and disconnect. Move the energy around, breathe deep, break a sweat, get your heart pumping, feel alive! Yoga is a phenomenal resource to use. It is available to you allllll the time!

I feel beyond blessed to have been given the gift of my yoga practice. As a Kripalu certified yoga instructor since 2010, not a day goes by that I take it for granted. The ability to turn your attention inward and focus on yourself is priceless. As I mentioned earlier in the book, this was my gateway to spirituality.

You get this one body, my friend. It's up to you to take good care of it!!

We hold trauma in our bodies on a cellular level. The different areas of the body have different associations. Releasing that trauma, held as tension, is referred to as somatic therapy. Soma=cell or "body."

There are different therapies to utilize when on the healing journey. "Top down" therapies include cognitive behavioral therapy (CBT) and dialectical behavioral therapy (DBT). These modalities move from the frontal lobes (cerebral cortex) of the brain and are more associated with thinking and speaking. They're primarily focused on retraining your thoughts. The efferent fibers conduct the input from the brain down through the body. Distortions in thinking come from distortions in affect (body's somatic "felt sense").

In trauma-informed care, it makes more sense to employ "bottom up" modalities to healing. The focus with this approach is more through the body's senses and feelings, hence referring to the body's "felt sense." This system of healing ties into the Polyvagal Theory because the focus is on the body's automatic responses. The area of the mammalian brain that develops earliest in life is called the primitive brain, the brain stem. Afferent fibers pass the input along, moving upwards from the body to the brain; we have more afferent fibers than efferent fibers. All our autonomic functions happen here, as well as our ability to be kept safe. It's all about survival, remember? This is where F/F/F/F unfolds. After trauma, you may get stuck in this mode, hyper-vigilant, constantly scanning for threats. Examples of ways to move through this response are yoga, dance, movement, mindfulness, EMDR (Eye Movement Desensitization Reprocessing), sensorimotor psychotherapy, progressive muscle relaxation, tai chi. Somatic experiencing aims to reprogram the sub-cortical part of the brain, including the amygdala, the brain's "alarm system" that goes hand-in-hand with neuroception. Through the experiencing, the body processes and integrates the trauma more efficiently so you're able to move through it all, instead of remaining stuck in the dysfunctional states.

IT IS NECESSARY to *get out of your head and into your body*! The body reacts, then the mind thinks. Remember, story follows form?? You can't change your thinking about something until you first identify how you feel about it. When you're in your head, you're likely overthinking. When you're in your body, you are sensing/feeling. THAT is where you want to be to connect to your intuition!! <u>Drop into your body often</u> and become mindful and aware of sensations and feelings.

For optimal, effective, long-term healing, a lovely combination of "top down" and "bottom up" therapies work best.

Lesson 21a: Personal Boundaries

Boundaries are what you will accept of another's words or actions. They are sometimes thought of as weapons, to be sure to put ourselves first. For those who have a difficult time saying "no" when you don't want to do something, learning about boundaries is very important.

Why personal boundaries??

For better relationships!! They keep people together in healthy ways by promoting respect, allowing us to work together not against each other in relationships.

Boundaries allow us to stay protected and connected to others.

Without healthy boundaries, feelings of resentment, disappointment, and betrayal are likely to occur. Feelings of enmeshment, overlap and co-dependency are common.

Enmeshment is a term used to describe a relationship that lacks boundaries and has pervasive or intrusive emotions with repeated cycles.

You often realize you have boundaries (or don't) when they've been crossed! To bring more awareness to this concept, start observing what offends you, makes you uncomfortable, and see if it's there are any patterns as far as who is prompting those feelings.

Lesson 21b: Boundary Styles

There are three main boundary styles, each with a purpose.

Porous: Will keep you connected not protected
- overshares personal information
- has a hard time saying "no" to requests from others
- over-involved in others' problems
- is dependent on opinions of others
- accepting of abuse/disrespect
- fears rejection when turning others down

Rigid: Will keep you protected not connected
- avoids intimacy and close relationships

- not likely to ask for help
- few close relationships
- may seem detached with romantic partners
- keeps others at a distance
- fear of rejection

Healthy: Connected and protected! Woot!!

- values others opinions
- won't compromise values for others
- shares personal information appropriately
- aware of personal wants and needs and is able to communicate them effectively
- accepting when others say "no"

Types of boundaries (invisible)

Physical

• Personal space/Proximity

• No forced hugs or touching: You decide who, how, where and when to be touched declining an invitation, or if traveling, possibly staying at a hotel instead of with friends or family

• Privacy

Emotional/Feelings/Mental

• To be able to separate mine and theirs

• Knowing your truth, your reality, beliefs, opinions

• Remembering: independent thoughts are healthy

• Can be difficult if you are prone to co-dependent relationships

Time

• Limiting time...attend an event for a certain amount of time and then leaving, e.g. staying for dinner but then going home after

Material
• Belongings: Lending things, e.g. someone borrows your car

Verbal
• Limiting conversations: Do not engage in certain topics of conversation, for example avoiding politics or religion

Sexual
• No hanky-panky when family is staying over or while staying at others' homes

In setting boundaries, it's important to understand that "the feel bads" are natural. This is a term Dr. Nicole LePera (IG: @the.holistic.psychologist) has used. It is very common to feel bad after you set a boundary and honor it. Though you KNOW it's necessary to set the boundary for your own safety and peace of mind, you still may get "the feel bads."It's a natural response, especially if you have previously been a people pleaser.

Assert the boundary, breathe deeply, soften your body, and sit in compassion. Be appreciative and consistent!!

When starting a new normal, a nice format to present the change is: "I know you're used to xyz, I would prefer abc." Ideally the person you're conveying this message to is receptive and supportive of honoring the change you're asking for. If they're not, that may be an indication of their level of respect for you (ultimately based on their level of respect for themselves).

Remember, the ones who get upset when you set the boundary are typically the ones benefitting from you not having any. No means No. You get to redefine the relationship. You get to decide if that type of relationship fits into your vision of your future.

Lesson 21c: Mantras to Support Boundary Setting

Mantras are tools for your own reassurance and mental recitation. When using mantras to support your own boundary setting, it is crucial to center yourself, remembering you are separate from the other person's reactions.

What is a mantra?

Traditionally, a mantra is a sacred utterance rooted in Sanskrit though here we are using English. The purpose of this repeated word or phrase is to call in a new energy. As an invocation, you are using the words to reverberate through your being so circumstances can shift and reprogram in your favor. A lot like positive affirmations.

Some beautiful examples are as follows:
- "I am safe to express my needs," then take a deep belly breath in and exhale to release tension and ground yourself
- "I have every right to feel what I'm feeling," taking a big breath in, let it out, relax and ground here, now
- "It is okay to be misunderstood," breathing in deeply, softening on the exhalation, be here, now.

- Any others you can think of that you may want to create for your own situation

WHICH BOUNDARY(-IES) FEEL THE MOST DIFFICULT TO YOU? WHAT DO YOU GET TO WORK ON WITH INTENTION?

Lesson 22: Attachment Theory

Okay, so LISTEN UP. This is another big one.

Like, a really BIG ONE. To me, probably the biggest lesson.

Attachment theory is a psychological and evolutionary theory concerning relationships among humans. The main tenent is that a young child needs to develop a healthy relationship with at least one primary caregiver for social and emotional development to occur "normally."

Early attachment experiences with primary caregivers are internalized into mental representations of self and others, thus shaping our models and how we cognitively, emotionally and behaviorally respond in intimate relationships.

Attachment style is thought to be stable and consistent throughout the lifespan though it can change with mental/cognitive/mindset training and reinforcing through secure attachments.

If one was known for having insecure attachments (anxious, avoidant: fearful or dismissive, disorganized) and is able to experience a secure attachment within a relationship lasting three years or longer it is said to affect every other relationship that individual has with others, in a positive way. This is referred to as an EARNED secure attachment. I seriously want to hand out trophies and gold medals for earning that!!!

The graphic on page 165 depicts the three main styles of attachments, though there really are four. I'll explain.

Attachment Styles

Anxious Attachment styles are also thought of as "preoccupied", which means that you obsess over the relationship. This attachment style is known for dysfunctional relational beliefs.

When anxious attachment is activated the person's coping strategies run the gamut from snooping, jealousy, attention-seeking behavior,

Understanding ATTACHMENT STYLES

@kara_karaoguz

ANXIOUS

- Desires a lot of closeness in the relationship
- Expresses insecurities- worried about rejection
- Gets caught up in the relationship
- Has a sensitive nervous system
- Seeks high levels of intimacy, approval and responsiveness from partner
- Acts out or exhibits "protest" behavior
- Unhappy when not in relationship
- Fears that little bumps in the relationship will lead to breakup
- Tend to become overly dependent on partner

AVOIDANT

- Sends mixed signals
- Devalues significant other
- Uses distancing strategies-emotionally and physically
- Doesn't make intentions clear
- Emotionally flat, unavailable, seemingly disconnected or disinterested
- Mistrustful
- Has difficulty communicating
- Isolated
- Unpredictable
- Doesn't want to get close to others-keeps loved ones at a distance
- Ambivalent about relationship

SECURE

- Confident
- Emotionally available, appropriately responsive to loved ones needs
- Non-reactive
- Healthy relationship bonds
- Comfortable with emotional intimacy and proximity-physical closeness
- Reliable and consistent
- Not afraid of commitment or dependency
- Communicates issues well, Naturally expresses feelings
- Closeness creates more closeness
- Leads with cooperation

www.karakaraoguz.com

positive/negative response to ambivalence, not caring or withdrawn once any fear is confirmed, and abandonment.

Those experiencing anxious attachments want more intimacy and commitment and if they anticipate avoidance and ambivalence from another they will experience fears of unworthiness and rejection. They seem to love their partner more than they love themselves. Constantly on the lookout for signs of rejection. Individuals with anxious attachment styles often disclose emotions and information

LEAN IN...

@kara_karaoguz

YOU MAY HAVE AN ANXIOUS ATTACHMENT STYLE IF:

- You prefer to be coupled in a relationship
- You desire more closeness and intimacy than your partner
- You crave your partners approval and are constantly chasing in attempts to get your needs met
- You have an intense fear of rejection if you don't go along with what your partner wants; you tend to people please (sometimes without knowing it)
- You're super dependent on the opinions of others, whether you want to admit it or not
- You opt to smooth things over as fast as possible after an argument, even if there is no resolution just so you don't have to feel the anxiety, unrest, turmoil, negative energy anymore
- You had a childhood in which your caregivers (likely your mom) were not as available as you wish they were
- You are really good at feeling other peoples feelings...you identify as an Empath

www.karakaraoguz.com

indiscriminately and tend to have porous boundaries.

Those who default to an anxious style of attachment may partake in "protest behavior." This looks like repeated calls, texts, video chats, following someone around when arguing, all to elicit a response from the less-engaged person. Evolutionarily speaking, this happens for our own survival. Let's say a baby chimp gets separated from its mama, it will "protest" with sounds and frantic gestures until the mama finds it and it feels safe again. We do that too, even as adults. There is a younger (unhealed) version of ourselves that comes forward when we are acting out. We thrive on the attention. Remember...survival. Plus, thinking back to the caveman days, our chances of surviving in a group or coupled together were greater than if one was alone. Your instincts are designed to help you feel safe and keep you alive. Period.

To support healing this style of attachment, inner child work does wonders. Just as I looked to the root of my issues (in Part I), you must go back to the source. There is a younger version of you who needs YOUR love and attention, not someone else's. Focus on the age that comes up for you when you're triggered within this style (often when in dynamic with another insecure style of attachment). Practice regulating your nervous system is clutch too. It is commonly the task of self-regulation, so pay special attention to that when studying the first part of this chapter (Lesson 19). Refer to your list of Glimmers and glimmer the shit out of yourself when you're feeling triggered.

Avoidant Attachment styles have two categories: Fearful and dismissive. In both cases they often experienced an early relationship with a primary caregiver who was unresponsive or entirely unavailable so they had to fend for themselves. Individuals with this attachment style have been shown there is little to no value in relationships and seek to distance themselves from intimacy due to discomfort with being so close to another person. The undercurrent is that "it is only safe to rely on myself."

Someone who is fearful avoidant has an intense need for closeness and also an intense fear of closeness. There is a need for approval. The dismissive avoidant has a need for independence. These two notions conflict and confuse the nervous system which ultimately leads to "freeze mode" or being in the dorsal vagal activation. This leads to immobility and disconnection.

Individuals with an avoidant attachment style (fearful and dismissive) feel overwhelmed when bombarded with too much emotion. They tend to shut down in argument. They often devalue their partner by making jokes or getting annoyed at dumb things like the way you drive, the way you eat, your appearance.

Those with avoidant attachments tend to focus on your faults. They will keep their partners at a certain distance on all levels (physically, emotionally among others). They get irritated or unnerved by too much closeness. The more partner A (likely an anxious attachment style) wants to be in close proximity, the more distant and dismissive partner B (avoidant) becomes. More on this in Lesson 23a.

If you have an avoidant style of attachment and are looking to move towards secure, increasing self-awareness is a great starting point. You're here, now. Reading this book, taking this new knowledge in. When you notice the desire to push back towards higher levels of intimacy, stop and breathe. Remind yourself that it's safe to be close. Focus on your partner's positive qualities rather than their flaws. Allow yourself to share (small) aspects of yourself that may feel vulnerable to you. Despite the urge to run away or escape intimate situations, practice gradually increasing your tolerance of the discomfort. If you are feeling a strong pull towards alone time, let your partner know that you need a minute and once you've had time to regroup, turn towards your partner even if it feels scary. Lean in.

Disorganized Attachment style is just as it sounds...they go between all the maladaptive, insecure styles. This is the FOURTH Style that is not depicted on the graphic (page 166) though you can see it's a combo of both anxious and avoidant. Very confusing, definitely indicative of some major trauma during upbringing.

In adulthood, coming to the realization that you want to change maladaptive attachment styles is very brave. It is possible though!! The key is to understand what is happening on a physiological level. It will all start to make sense, putting the puzzle pieces together, connecting the dots!!

It is common to show up differently in relationships with different people. Some relationships you may present with an insecure attachment style while some you may feel entirely secure and confident. Your feeling of safety weighs heavily here. If you are feeling unsafe for any reason, you will likely default to an insecure style.

WHICH ATTACHMENT STYLE SOUNDS THE MOST LIKE YOU? REMEMBER, YOU CAN SHOW UP DIFFERENTLY IN DIFFERENT RELATIONSHIP DYNAMICS.

ARE YOU ABLE TO MAKE THE CONNECTION BETWEEN YOUR UPBRINGING/RELATIONSHIPS WITH EARLY CAREGIVERS AND HOW YOU SHOW UP IN RELATIONSHIPS NOW?

HOW ARE YOU ABLE TO MEET YOUR OWN NEEDS TO SOOTHE AND HEAL ANYTHING YOU LOOK FOR EXTERNALLY, WHEN IN RELATIONSHIPS WITH OTHERS?

Lesson 23a: Codependency

Sometimes codependency is referred to as "Enmeshment," first mentioned in Lesson 21a. This is complete entanglement with another. Codependency is losing yourself when coupled with someone, or even with a family member, friend, child, loved one.

When we take attachment styles into consideration (to me that's what it boils down to), I prefer to call this dynamic the Anxious-Avoidant dyad. It consists of having a push-pull dynamic. For the anxiously attached person, there is a major fear of abandonment. Low self-worth comes into play and the need for external validation and approval is off the charts. For the avoidantly attached, they feel smothered by their partners need for reassurance and they push away. Both insecure attachment styles feed off one another, in a sense and contribute to a negative, unhealthy, toxic dynamic. It's an awful cycle. I lived it for too long. Never again.

Once you start to really take a look at this, you'll see lots of overlap of unhealed trauma, core wounds, insecure attachments, lack of healthy boundaries, etc. Refer to the graphic on the next page for the breakdown.

"Codependency"
BROKEN DOWN

@kara_karaoguz

PARTNER A

- Anxious Attachment Style-very "preoccupied" with the relationship, seeks high levels of intimacy, approval and responsiveness from partner, acts out in "protest behavior"-ex repeated texts/calls, desire to get partners attn
- Core Wounds of unworthiness, fear of rejection, abandonment "issues"
- Tend to have Porous Boundaries-overshare personal info, gets caught up in other persons stuff, people pleaser, is dependent on opinion of others
- Nervous System dys-regulation-Sympathetic Activation Fight/Flight/FAWN (intense need to smooth things over though no resolution)
- Associate as an Empath

PARTNER B

- Avoidant Attachment Style-sends mixed signals, devalues partner, emotionally flat and distant, has difficulty communicating emotions, often ambivalent about the relationship, feels trapped in relationships, unpredictable, selfish
- Core Wounds fear of neglect, rejection, fear of abandonment, expectations of others, False sense of self (artificial persona to protect self)
- Tend to have Rigid Boundaries-avoids intimacy and closeness, not likely to ask for help, may seem detached, keeps distance
- Nervous System dys-regulation-Dorsal Vagal Activation leading to immobilization, shut down, retreat mode
- Traits of Narcissist (though really hella insecure)

www.karakaraoguz.com

Lesson 23b: 🔗Empath/Narcissist dynamic🔗

Are you familiar with this??

Brief overview:

Narcissist=
- inability to handle criticism
- inflated sense of self
- sense of entitlement
- grandiose view of everything…it's all exaggerated
- need for admiration
- exploits others, could care less about other people's feelings
- bullies/intimidates others

Empath=
- able to feel other's pain (mostly emotional, sometimes physical too)
- may take on other's emotions
- can feel the vibe in the room: it matters
- you understand people
- others confide in you
- you are calming to others
- you love animals…and I mean LOVE
- can't watch the news or horror movies-human tragedy can really take you down
- you KNOW when others are lying

✦ I identify as an Empath, obvi ✦

Now…onto the dynamic…

It's said that narcissists are drawn to Empaths because of their light.

There is a "toxic relationship" between the two, extremely

dysfunctional and damaging to the Empath.

Empaths are healers and want to "fix" the wounded narc when really the narcissist is very manipulative, evil, cold hearted, blah blah blah.

My thoughts are this....

1. It's all rooted in unhealed trauma. All of it. Combo of "nature"/ genes (read: passed down as generational trauma stored in DNA) and "nurture"/environmental molding...trauma, more generational shit passed down, shitty boundaries: rigid or porous, no structure/too much

2. When we vilify and create distinctions, we get sucked into the mentality of SEPARATION. Us vs Them. We are all human. Every single person has built their own defenses to keep themselves alive. View self and others through the lens of compassion 🩶

3. THIS IS EXTREMELY DISEMPOWERING TO EMPATHS.

If you are an Empath and have found yourself in this type of dynamic, blaming the asshole narcissist you chose to be with GIVES YOUR POWER AWAY.

I challenge you to turn your attention to yourself:

What boundaries did you have in place in the relationship?

How do you really feel about yourself to allow another to manipulate you? To hurt you repeatedly? All while you stood by this person.

Look at your self-esteem, self-respect, and your boundaries.

Learn more and protect yourself!!

Remember, when we blame others it is disempowering.

It's your own responsibility...

...your ABILITY to RESPOND....

Practice your response to bullshit, not impulsive reactions. Become aware of the patterns that no longer serving you and that prevent you from moving forward. Do the work covered in this book, reach out for support and you WILL overcome this pattern.

Lesson 23c: Trauma Bonds

This is a very interesting concept to me. Trauma bonds happen when you know you need to move on from a relationship with someone that is unhealthy yet you are still drawn to them. You continue to reach out or engage, despite the fact that it may be really unproductive conversation. The need to engage arises just like a drug addict feels the need to use again. It is a physiological response, neuro-biologically you may feel like you HAVE to have contact with the person.

Much like the codependent traits, there is a push-pull dynamic. Neither partner feels safe. One or both are constantly "walking on eggshells." There is no open, honest communication with regards to individual needs and emotions.

With trauma bonds, there is an emotional addiction where there is chaos and a major fear of abandonment (anxious attachment, anyone??) which create the illusion and façade of sexual chemistry. There is a "love/hate" dynamic with a very strong nervous system activation.

These bonds are rooted in both of your traumas, insecurities, unhealthy coping patterns. It is likely that you experienced a similar dynamic with a caregiver in your upbringing so this feels comfortable to you; it feels like home in the most effed up, dysfunctional sense. I lived this for awhile. It was not fun. There is hope to overcome!! It is important to work closely with a therapist, mentor, experienced/ educated coach to help support you through this if you are in it.

Lesson 24: Cycle Breaker

The Karmic cycle ends when you decide to no longer participate.

You get to decide how much you will tolerate. We teach people how to treat us. In order to gain confidence to set and honor healthy boundaries, you GET to know your worth. You must be aware of your value and refuse to settle for anything less.

One of the goals in relationships with others is moving towards Secure Attachments.

Secure Attachments are marked by intimacy, closeness, commitment, trust, support, constructive conflict management skills.

People with these attachments are more open and positive in their beliefs about romantic love, have increased levels of self-disclosure, maintain a healthy balance between closeness and independence.

Those with secure attachments are comfortable displaying interest and affection. They have little concern about avoidance or anxiety. Those with secure attachments are not worried about rejection or feelings of anxiety within the relationship. It's easy for them to get close to others; they're comfortable depending on others and having others depend on them.

Secure attachment peeps aren't worried about being abandoned or about someone getting too close. Indicators of partner satisfaction include partner responsiveness and emotional engagement.

Without these, relationship quality drops and there are increased rates of divorce.

When the couple dyad consists of anxious and avoidant attachments, dissatisfaction is high, there is increased conflict, jealousy, distrust, worries about rejection and unworthiness, obsessive, dependent love, clinging and controlling. Ugh. No Thanks.

Stages of becoming Securely Attached *Yes, Please!!!*

- Cultivate a desire to change
- Have an awareness of ANS defaults and empathic tendencies: Regulate, Regulate, Regulate (practice impulse control, discipline in responses, be mindful of self and other)
- Develop a new vision for the future, see the possibilites
- Learn new tools and techniques for your Empath Backpack
- Practice the shit out of the aforementioned steps!!!! (new responses, skills, habits, tendencies, patterns)

Lesson 25a: Core Wounds

Holy shnickies!! This is a lot!!! This topic could be a whole book in and of itself!!! For the sake of brevity, I consolidated Core Wounds into one lesson.

Core wounds are emotional scars inflicted in childhood and can determine quality of life as adults. They hold a deep level of pain. Oftentimes the caregiver is deficient in their own healing, they don't realize they're hurting a child. This can include neglect, abuse, maltreatment, emotional unavailability. Generational trauma comes into play here!

So the wounding happens, which leads to deeply ingrained beliefs that perpetuate damage. These beliefs could be that you're not good enough, you're incompetent, worthless, no one likes you, you're stupid, you may experience self-hatred, etc.

Honestly, when looking at relationships, it is very clear to me what each person has their own wounding around. Ya know when couples are arguing and then they go, "I don't even know what we're fighting about!" It's the core wounds that get slashed open. Until you have more awareness around your own wounding, these conflicts will flare up at the drop of a dime.

The challenge with the core wounding of shame, guilt, mistrust, fear of rejection and/or abandonment is to be able to bring them to light and remove their power over you! Sometimes we push it away because you're afraid of more hurt. But remember: Shat you resist persists. We have to feel it to heal it.

When healing these core wounds, it's sort of touch and go. You don't have to dig it all out at once. It's important to get right in there and recognize the patterns, call yourself out, and be held accountable for change. Reprogramming the thoughts and feelings is essential. Reclaim your sacred self! This healing helps you on the path of ascension!!

Lesson 25b: Shame

Shame is a powerful emotion that can cause people to feel defective, unacceptable, even damaged beyond repair. It's a sense that you are fundamentally flawed. The focus is on your sense of BEING (John Bradshaw).

Feelings of shame can begin as early as fifteen months of age. The sense that you want to disappear, you feel worthless, are taking up other people's time, wasting space, that you're inherently defective, you blame yourself, feel angry, embarrassed, humiliated.

Shame is internalized. There is a fear of rejection. You may feel tempted to disconnect from others and avoid the pain or shame of them leaving first. Those caught up in addictions often live in a cycle of shame.

Overcoming sexual shame can also be a challenge, especially for those of us with a history of (childhood) sexual abuse, assault, rape, incest. It is important to look at early programming around sex and intimacy in this sense, give it a voice, then work to re-program more positive associations, releasing the shame once and for all!!

Being able to share with others that you carry the core wound of shame does wonders to decrease its power over you! Who knew??!?

The beauty of gaining this awareness is that we can start to develop shame resilience! The **antidote to shame** starts with self-compassion. To be able to shift feelings of shame we have to identify situations that provoke feelings of shame leading to dynamics that trigger you. No self-criticism allowed! Allow yourself to pursue relationships and nurture connections and a sense of belonging with others. Sharing negative, self-critical thoughts with another person is one of the best ways to combat shame. Sharing vulnerability and admitting to these feelings allows you to rewire the messages of shame and let them go.

Lesson 25c: Guilt

Guilt is a psychological discomfort about something that you've done that's against your unrealistically high standards. Guilt comes about when you act in ways that break the standards of behavior developed in early childhood to please an adult. We can experience guilt as early as ages three to six. We stay this way until we correct irrational beliefs.

Guilt has more of a DOING essence (John Bradshaw); Based off of a behavior.

Again, the beauty in really looking at the guilt core wounding is that we get to focus on resilience and healing!

One of the primary **antidotes to guilt** is self-compassion: knowing that we all have a combination of strengths and weaknesses. Other antidotes to guilt are experiencing a connection with others, joining a self-help group, seeking forgiveness and "righting the wrong." There is so much power in the repair of a conflict; this leads to tremendous healing. You have to face the behavior (whatever the fuck-up was) and take responsibility for the harm. It's necessary to change destructive behavior and attitudes that created the harmful behavior. Reclaim your wholeness and heal the relationship with other people affected by your wrongful doing.

Lesson 25d: Fear of Rejection and/or Fear of Abandonment

These core wounds tie in with one another and tend to overlap.

If you are experiencing these wounds, you feel it all on the inside. It is common to view the world through the filter of your scars. You typically undervalue yourself, try to attain perfection, tend to want to run away from conflict or problems. This is often because you were rejected as a child. There is always that feeling until the wound is healed.

Again, in bringing awareness to these wounds the beauty is that we can identify **the antidotes**, the healing involved in closing them for good!!

Antidotes to healing Fear of Rejection +/or Fear of Abandonment:

- work on forgiveness for self and possibly others
- value oneself
- appreciate all you are
- have a creative outlet
- get physical, move your body every single day
- practice radical acceptance
- get yo ass out in nature as often as possible!!!
- feel confidence without the need for approval
- putting yourself first
- embody self-compassion
- understanding attachment styles
- put boundaries in place
- know your worth!
- take warm, soothing epsom salt baths often
- listen to your favorite music
- nourish your body: eat clean and stay hydrated
- accept the wound as part of the self; the only authority or control we have is acceptance of ourselves...don't reject self
- invest in yourself
- watch your internal dialogue and only speak kindly of yourself

IDENTIFY YOUR CORE WOUNDS AND LIMITING BELIEFS. THIS IS FUNDAMENTAL TO BECOME AWARE OF THESE BLOCKS!!! THESE ARE MAJOR BARRIERS TO LOVE, ABUNDANCE, PROSPERITY, HAPPINESS!! THESE BLOCKS DO NOT ALLOW YOU TO RECEIVE ALL THAT'S AVAILABLE TO YOU. IT IS ESSENTIAL TO SPEAK TO THESE MISTRUTHS, CLEAR THEM, RELEASE THEM, SHARE THEM WITH SOMEONE YOU TRUST TO REMOVE THEIR HOLD ON YOU!! REMEMBER, IT'S A PRACTICE OF OVERCOMING, HANDLING YOURSELF WITH COMPASSION/ SOFTNESS/LOVE, AND REPROGRAMMING!!

Lesson 26: The Void and Shadow Work

When you have a history of trauma or abuse it is not uncommon to feel the void and then have shadow work to do. The integration of self and being able to transmute the darkness to light is where the magic happens!

Core wounds become very loud when we feel this void.

It drives the nonstop need for love, approval, validation, acceptance from others. It sometimes feels like it's never enough... That you always need more!!

The shadow is rooted in the unconscious self. That darkness is born out of your core wounding. So all of this goes hand-in-hand. Much like healing core wounds, it is so important to share this darkness with another. Handle yourself with care and continue to check in!

You know, that pit in your stomach? The emptiness in your lower abdomen? In your heart? The need to fill that space in any possible way to distract yourself from that discomfort?

You may temporarily fill that void by:

❌ buying things, spending money, accumulating *stuff*, getting farther and farther into debt

✖ drinking to numb those feelings

✖ turning to other substances to check out and not feel

✖ overindulging in food

✖ cutting yourself

✖ having mindless sex with strangers or meaningless sex with people you may know

✖ disconnecting from yourself in any other way possible

Then you get really comfortable with carrying more bullshit than is necessary:

✖ thousands of $$ in debt just sitting on credit cards or loans

✖ a baseline of alcohol or drugs in your system

✖ the extra weight on your figure

Any chance you get you try to escape the void... until you get sick of your own shit.

Sooner or later you HAVE to sit with the discomfort. With the emptiness. The void.

And little by little you start to turn it around... you start *showing up* for yourself, loving yourself, being kind to yourself, nurturing yourself!!

You have to feel it to heal it. The only way out is through it.

You come to realize that all that OUT THERE will never fill you.

You have to fill yourself, from the inside out!! Only you can do this.

It takes practice to become aware of your own thoughts and behaviors, stop the negative self talk, reprogram your thoughts with positive affirmations and completely SHIFT YOUR MINDSET around what works for you.

Know you are not alone!! Sooooo many people are running from themselves.

When you get to a point where you're ready for change, line up your supports, surround yourself with positivity and others who are on a similar mission: to HEAL themselves. There are lots of like-minded souls in my private Facebook Group: Intuitive Self Healers. Join us!

The beauty in all of this is coming to realize the gifts that are born out of the trauma and darkness.

Antidotes to dealing with The Void: self-compassion, boundaries, gratitude, reprogramming, patching the heart so your tank doesn't leak!! Surround yourself with those who will lift you up. Energy work: cranial-sacral therapy, Reiki, EFT, hypnosis, support groups, personal development books

DO YOU KNOW THIS "VOID" I SPEAK OF?? CAN YOU RECOGNIZE YOUR SHADOW AND BEGIN TO INTEGRATE AND TRANSMUTE THAT ENERGY TO LIGHT? HAVE YOU PULLED ANY LESSONS OUT OF THE SHADOW SELF? CAN YOU BELIEVE YOUR OWN STRENGTH AND RESILIENCE?? WHEN YOU IDENTIFY YOUR SHADOW, PAUSE AND TAKE THREE DEEP BELLY BREATHS. NOTICE WHAT YOU ARE FEELING. NOTICE WHERE IN YOUR BODY YOU ARE FEELING IT. BREATHE THROUGH IT, REMIND YOURSELF OF YOUR STRENGTH. OFFER ONLY COMPASSION AND ACCEPTANCE TO THAT PART OF YOURSELF THAT IS CALLING FOR ATTENTION. NO JUDGMENTS! KEEP SHOWING UP!!

Chapter 10

Unconditional Love

"Love isn't a state of perfect caring, it is an active noun like struggle. To love someone is to strive to accept that person exactly the way he or she is, right here and now."

-Fred Rogers

When I think about our reason for being here, in this physical body, on Planet Earth, I believe that its for two reasons. One, for our **soul to grow, evolve, expand, and ascend** to higher planes of consciousness. To increase awareness of self and others. And two, to learn **Unconditional Love**.

These two beliefs are the foundation for everything I do in this life. As a woman, mom, teacher, author, coach, companion, lover, friend, relative. Being able to understand ourselves and others is the gateway to reasons we are here.

I am a fan of Dr. Gary Chapman's work when it comes to understanding love. He is the author of *The 5 Love Languages*. Below you'll find more detailed descriptions of each of the languages. You can take a test online to see which is most aligned with your expressions of love.

Lesson 27: Be a Conscious Partner

Holla, The 5 Love Languages by Gary Chapman, Ph.D

Words of Affirmation

Gives and receives love through encouragement, affirmations, appreciation, empathizing with another, and listening actively. Ideas for how to love someone who primarily speaks this love language: Send a surprise note, a nice text, give them a card, brag to others about your spouse, speak words that build security, offer encouragement authentically and often. Stay away from non-constructive criticism and ignoring, not recognizing or appreciating their efforts.

Physical Touch

Gives and receives love through physical contact, touch, and uses nonverbal body language as a means to communicate. Things to do to help show your love for someone who communicates with this love language: hug often, kiss, massage, hold hands, show physical affection regularly, really make intimacy a thoughtful priority. Stay away from offering affection coldly, neglecting physical needs, or going a long time without having any sexual intimacy.

Receiving Gifts 🎁

Gives and receives love through their thoughtful action, showing that the significant other is a priority. Things you can do if your loved one speaks this love language: give thoughtful gifts and offer kind gestures, even if they're very small, express gratitude when receiving a gift from them, surprise them. Stay away from forgetting special occasions or anniversaries, or unenthusiastically receiving a gift.

Quality Time

Gives and receives love through uninterrupted focused conversations, one-on-one time is very important. To show your love for someone who speaks their love language is quality time. Create special moments together, turn off electronics, plan date nights, start a hobby together, take walks and do small things with your significant other, be as present as possible, enjoy a getaway together.

Stay away from distractions when you're spending time together, or long bouts of 1:1 time.

Acts of Service

Gives and receive through helping others with tasks and actions. Things to do to show your love: Do chores together, cook a meal together, switch the laundry, different things that will help alleviate some of the stress of the daily workload. Stay away from not following through on tasks or letting others take precedent over your actions toward your partner.

Viewing your **Triggers as Teachers**… relationships will reveal the deep wounds you have in order to bring them to light so you can heal them!! Your triggers are your deep hurts reflected back to you!! There is gratitude in that!! Remember, it is of the utmost importance to create **safety** for yourself and another.

Be a conscious partner (when abuse is not part of the equation):

- Get curious, not defensive
- Listen with your heart instead of your head
- See the wounded inner child that may come out during conflict
- Replace criticism with praise, focus on gratitude
- See conflict as an opportunity to connect and grow
- Hold space for one another
- Prioritize play and laughter

- Be safe, seen, heard, understood and loved
- Accept this person as is

Based on the previous content, do you know which are your primary languages? (You can take a test online if you simply search it) Are you able and willing to show up as a Conscious Partner when in relationship?

Lesson 28: Holding Space, Be Present

This is important for us, in relations with others and for others in relations with us. Think of reciprocity. Both support one another. This is a sacred healthy masculine ability. More on sacred energies to come in future lessons.

To "hold space" for another is to simply bear witness to someone else's experience. To be there, fully, with your entire presence. All hands + hearts on deck.

To hold space is to have no judgments, no need to fix them or change the outcome. It's important to resist the urge to offer one's own experience, as a means to connect. What they're going through isn't about you.

To hold space is to offer unconditional love, awareness, attention and support. Just BE with the person who is in need. Just BE with the brave soul who is in the throes of potential pain + suffering, who is wanting change and is willing to do the work, who is "going through it" as I say, and truly honor their experience.

When we hold others in a spacious beautiful container, there is a feeling of safety. It allows others to feel heard and acknowledged. In this container, there are no feelings of shame, inadequacies, inferiority or doubt. Those on the receiving end are free to be themselves and feel full acceptance. This is where true healing happens.

It requires patience and the prioritization of things. In my roles as a mom, coach, birth doula, and RN the people I am with come first. They are my priority when I'm wearing that hat 🎩 👑.

Of course, it is vital that we hold space for ourselves before we are able to show up fully (holding space) for others. Do the work.

Lesson 29: The Importance of Repair in Relationships

When coupled in relationships, you'll inevitably encounter conflict and, naturally, the need for repair.

If there is a pattern of conflict with no repair, the chances of the relationship standing the test of time are highly unlikely.

I don't feel like enough emphasis is placed on the REPAIR (could be my own projections based on my own history with conflict rez, who knows?!) so I wanted to be sure to dedicate a whole lesson to it.

It's important for both parties involved to take turns leaning into initiating repair after conflict; to alternate "being the bigger person." If one is constantly the only one to lean in first, this creates an imbalance and it's likely that resentment could build.

Before initiating the repair, it is so important to take time for yourself to reflect on how you're feeling in the face of the conflict, and what you need to get your needs met. Sometimes this happens hours after the disagreement. Sometimes it happens during during the clash and the repair can be efficient.

Check in with the sensations in your body, noticing without judgment. Remember all you just read about the nervous system and our need for self-regulation (and ultimately co-regulation when the repair happens).

Allow yourself to become the witness and observe what you're experiencing without any judgment. And simply BREATHE. This is the practice!! Use the tools that have already been shared.

Some suggestions of what to say once you've both had time and are ready to discuss are:

- "I know we were both having a hard time moving through that before, how about we try again?"
- "Now that we have both had some time to think about things, do you want to share your thoughts/feelings?"
- " I know we were both really hurt earlier and I would like to connect so it doesn't fester"

To offer a clear outline of what to include when you do start talking about the issue, it's important to mention the following:

- In reflecting on things, I understand I was feeling...
- This was such a trigger for me because...
- In the future, moving forward I would like to handle things differently by...
- It would be helpful and supportive if you could do (xyz) differently...

It is so important to maintain an awareness of your self during the conflict and during the repair. **This is about you.** If you have a tendency to get caught up in the other person, as previously mentioned, be cognizant of that and work to change the patterns. All of this is practice!

In terms of the **5 Love Languages** by Gary Chapman Ph.D, speaking to each of the love languages in order to repair after conflict, this is what I think warrants attention:

For those whose primary love language is *Words of Affirmation*... speak words that build security, be sure to offer a sincere apology.

For those whose primary love language is *Acts of Service*... make conscious behavior changes that have been requested through the conflict.

For those whose primary love language is *Receiving Gifts*... write a note to apologize or offer a small token of love.

For those whose primary love language is *Quality Time*... make eye contact, listen actively with empathy, avoid interrupting, practice reiterating the last three words that are said.

For those whose primary love language is *Physical Touch*... hold each other without saying anything, cuddle together in bed, have at least five minutes of skin-to-skin therapy (no sex required though...ya know...).

I personally think all those suggestions for repair are relevant, no matter what your style of love language is!!! Consider printing them or creating your own list of ideas to pull from when the need for Repair arises, at least until it is more of a common practice.

Also remember the importance of your boundaries here!! You can go back and review anytime!!

HOW DO YOU FEEL ABOUT CONFLICT? HOW DO YOU FEEL ABOUT REPAIR? DO YOU HAVE A CONSCIOUS REPAIR PRACTICE IN PLACE? DID YOU DO THE INTERNET SEARCH TO TAKE THE 5 LOVE LANGUAGES QUIZ? CAN YOU SEE THESE SUGGESTIONS FOR REPAIR SUPPORTING YOUR LOVE LANGUAGE(S)?

Lesson 30: Sacred Masculine/Feminine Energies

I cannot stress this enough: We all have BOTH masculine and feminine energies within us, no matter the biological gender.

Though it is of the UTMOST importance (if the relationship is heterosexual) for a woman to align with a healthy, masculine man (not in the rah rah toxic, bullying vibe, more so in the confident, poised, protective energy).

If a woman has had a male parental figure who was experiencing his own wounding, (emotionally or physically) unavailable, neglectful, not ever present, etc., she may struggle to trust the masculine energy of another man...

Until she heals herself!!

She's likely to be very much in her empowered masculine energy leaving her sacred feminine energy in the dust.

This looks like constantly planning, doing, pushing, action, being seen as the strong one for everyone else, not believing that your male partner will follow through so you end up doing xyz anyways, overthinking... all this PLUS the Unhealthy, Wounded Feminine traits (see graphic on page 200).

If a woman has to take on masculine roles such as controlling, anticipating danger, worrying, taking action and making things happen then it becomes very difficult for the man to embody that energy. Instead, the man will shift into his feminine, whether empowered or wounded.

I'm not saying you can't take action, ladies. I am offering that you allow yourself to surrender, to trust, to flow, to be led, to give way. It is an art to surrender.

Understanding *Balance* Of Energies

@kara_karaoguz

Healthy, Empowered Masculine	Healthy, Empowered Feminine
• Confident-knows self	• Has a deep desire to let go, doesn't
• Must lead self before attempting to lead another	want to worry, plan, make decisions
• Takes the lead-gives directions, uses commands, prioritizes partners needs and wants	• Enjoys having wants/needs/desires take care of and explored
• Conveys deep presence-Holds Space like a Mutha!!	• Able to follow directions, flow, surrender, soften, trust, open,
• Responsible for the foundation of trust and grounding, protective, Valor and strength	receive, let go of need to control
• Moves from Heart center	• Willing to explore and be led
	• Moves from Heart center

Unhealthy, Wounded Masculine	Unhealthy, Wounded Feminine
• Controlling and Immature	• Feels unworthy
• Bullying/Intimidation	• Feels shameful
• Fear-based	• Doesn't speak truth
• Manipulative	• Inauthentic
• Domineering	• Says "I'm sorry" all the time
• Insecure, unworthy	• Doesn't understand boundaries
• Withdraws, Avoids	or has none
• Aggressive or emotionally vacant	• Looking outward to be saved
• Insensitive	• Overly emotional, nagging, panicky
• Shaming	• Deep sense of not being seen
• Uncommunicative	

www.karakaraoguz.com

Are you constantly attracting or in relationship with a man who is emotionally unavailable or distant, sending mixed signals, not motivated to take action, not communicating very well or you're questioning whether he's choosing you or not!!!?!

This guy has his own wounding but we're not gonna focus on that!! That's not up to you to "correct" his shit. It's on him.

If that sounds familiar and you're still here reading, in order to shift the dynamics in your relationship or attract a more aligned partner, then you have to do your OWN healing work with the Wounded Masculine.

Heal yourself first!! Shift your own frequency. The first step is AWARENESS!

Once it's healed in you then it'll be reflected back to you in your partnership or whoever you're attracting to you.

If you are constantly chasing love, acceptance, convincing another to want to be with you, waiting to be chosen, etc. etc. your feminine is wounded. If that piques your curiosity, you may benefit from looking into a mother wound. A lot of times, there is ancestral trauma. Unhealed beliefs or barriers to love passed down from generation to generation.

For those of us with a history of trauma or abuse IT CAN BE VERY DIFFICULT to loosen the reigns and give over that sense of power over and trust the Sacred Masculine Energy of another. It takes practice. If you have ever had to lead your own life so as to not be disappointed then the concept of being led may seem foreign, and it may cause anxiety! Do your best not to get caught up here.

It is a practice to be led, to trust, to surrender, etc. You will naturally do that when you feel safe and taken care of, held in the sacred masculinity.

UNDERSTANDING *Sexual* POLARITY
THE BALANCE OF ENERGIES

@kara_karaoguz

Masculine

- Confident- knows self, enjoys exploration with another and helping them explore themselves
- Must lead self before attempting to lead another
- Takes the lead, gives direction, uses commands, prioritize partners needs and wants depending on desires
- Conveys a deep presents for self and partner-eye contact, breathing, body/touch, language
- Is still and aware, able to hold space
- Responsible for the foundation of trust and grounding
- Moves from the heart center

Feminine

- A deep desire to let go, doesn't want to worry, plan, make decisions
- Enjoys having wants/needs/longings/desires taken care of and explored
- Able to follow directions, flow, surrender, soften, trust, open, receive, let go of the need to control
- Willing to be explore or be told how to explore another
- Feeling into where they're being led- take me anywhere you want to go, for own pleasure or for self
- Can be a challenge to surrender and trust another
- Moves from the heart center

ADDITIONAL NOTES:
SAFETY FIRST-ESPECIALLY IF THERE IS A HX OF TRAUMA
WE ALL HAVE BOTH ENERGIES, REGARDLESS OF GENDER,
IMPORTANT TO ALTERNATE ROLES WITH PARTNER

WHAT ARE YOUR THOUGHTS ON THE CONCEPT OF SACRED
MASCULINE/FEMININE ENERGY? DOES THE CONCEPT OF
SEXUAL POLARITIES MAKE SENSE? ARE YOU READY TO
EMBODY THEM?

Lesson 31a: Mindsets

Our thoughts and emotions are known to loop around one another and have a sort of snowball effect. Bring to mind the cycle of how you think and feel; see how this becomes your active state of being. When you keep thinking the same thoughts, you'll experience the same patterns, then you'll automatically think and feel a certain way.

In the case of past traumas, there seems to be a residue of sorts that permeates and clouds current day thinking. Past experiences of fear or inferiority (or really any of the core wounds) end up dictating your perceptions. Because of your past, you may be comfortable with emotions such as sadness, pain, grief, anxiety, unworthiness, or frustration. You may feel worry or mistrust of all those you come into contact with, regardless of how respectful and aligned with their morals and dignity they may be. If these sorts of emotions are driving your thoughts and influencing your choices, behaviors and experiences then life will stay the same forever. It will be like Groundhog's Day. No matter who you are in relations with, remove the person's face in your pictures and replace it with the next, every single relationship will play out the same. Reruns of the past. Until you make the conscious effort to change. You must do the work. You must cut your shit thinking off at the pass...having the awareness to not go down the rabbit hole of worst-case scenario, or getting caught up in the what-ifs. Consciously choosing to focus on what you KNOW to be true of the current situation will be a very therapeutic, healing practice for you. Also, incorporating in new ways of thinking.

When we move from the awareness of Gratitude, Prosperity, Joy, and Abundance our lives are sooooo much more fulfilling! These are all ways of viewing life, through these lenses.

Remember, everything is energy!

You get to **CHOOSE** what you focus on.

Where your attention goes, energy flows!! What you appreciate, appreciates!

As mentioned before, INTENTION is vital.

As you move through your day, be aware of all you are grateful for, all the prosperity around you (something as simple as an abundance of creamer for your coffee!), alllllll the things that bring you JOY, and the onslaught of abundance available to you when you really start paying attention and expressing appreciation!!

This is FOR REAL!!!

Lesson 31b: Gratitude

According to the New Oxford American Dictionary, gratitude is the quality of being thankful, a readiness to show appreciation for and to return kindness.

It's a rich emotion!!

It's like a muscle: the more you work it, the stronger it gets!! Energy flows where attention goes!

Why gratitude?

We are energetic beings!! Remember, the chart of emotional frequencies in Lesson 6?

Energy CAN get stuck or be stagnant in your chakras, your main energy centers.

Law Of Attraction: like attracts like! This is the key to manifesting: the emotional state and the ability to trust and surrender your wishes!

Don't question at all, feel sure that it's yours just as sure as your breath is yours. Know that it's here!

Health is so important to our entire lives! Good health is such a crucial thing in our lives. Without our health we really have nothing! Each day we're given the gift of life. Giving thanks for the health you are receiving is essential!

Health is wealth. Often our health is taken for granted until we're sick or something worse. Remember: *Move. Your. Body. Every day!*

Gratitude in Relationships

In one way or another we are constantly engaged in a relationship, with ourselves and with others!! It's no surprise that when we feel appreciated we do more, we show up more and engage more. We're more responsive to the other person's needs and in romantic situations it brings a couple closer. Gratitude strengthens our intimate relationships and allows us to create and hold onto those close bonds. I'm talking about more than a simple "thank you"!!

We get matched up with those who mirror back parts of ourselves that need healing. Remember... vibrations...frequencies... and our subconscious beliefs come into play here.

"We don't see things as they are, we see things as we are."
-Anais Nin

Relationships are our greatest spiritual assignment. Soul Contracts are coming up in the next chapter. These relationships bring darkness to light, to the surface, and can magnify whatever is really going on inside of you.

Viewing our triggers are our treasures. The gems, the gold....that's where our WORK resides! When we notice and acknowledge our triggers, this allows us a tremendous opportunity to break free from old patterns, insecurities, and fears. I introduced this concept in Part I when sharing about my own treasures.

The KEY is that your Significant Other is a safe place to land!! If not, Thank You, Next!!

Depending on the attachment styles you have established from your early caregivers, if you experience anxious, insecure, or avoidant styles these will undoubtably be revealed!!

Even if you experienced insecure attachments in childhood, these attachments are malleable! You can turn it around. Remember, earned secure attachments!!?!

We get hurt in relationships and we heal in relationships!! There is hope!!

Lesson 31c: Neuroplasticity

This is the ability to rewire our brains! When we are consciously thinking new thoughts, we are creating new neural pathways. What fires together wires together. By focusing on gratitude, abundance, joy, prosperity, you are rewiring the neural pathways.

Make it a habit! A habit of feeling grate-FULLness!!

One of the easiest ways to rewire the brain and create new neural pathways is with **"I am" statements** and Positive Affirmations. I am statements are powerful declarations. Whatever you put after "I am" shapes your reality so choose carefully! Be aware of your self talk and what you are putting out to the Universe. The same is true for Positive Affirmations.

Positive Affirmations

All is mirrored and reflected back to you.

Positive affirmations are phrases or mantras that you repeat to yourself, which describe a specific outcome. When you first start creating them, they may feel false! The purpose is to be able to reprogram your thoughts... with repetition your subconscious mind starts to believe them and they become your reality!

When taking conscious steps to create a new normal for yourself (in a positive way!) it is vital that you stay committed to the practice. You can write out positive affirmations in present tense on Post-its and place them all around the home, write them in your journal, have them in your vehicle, anywhere you can view them... saturate your mind with the goodness until you start believing them.

WHAT DOES GRATITUDE MEAN TO YOU?

WHAT DOES GRATITUDE FEEL LIKE IN YOUR BODY? DESCRIBE THE SENSATIONS.

IN WHAT WAYS ARE YOU GRATEFUL FOR YOUR HEALTH AT THIS TIME?

LIST ALL THE SYSTEMS OF THE BODY (THAT YOU CAN THINK OF) AND EXPRESS GRATITUDE, STATING WHY YOU ARE THANKFUL FOR EACH!!

DO YOU SEE HOW YOUR TRIGGERS ARE YOUR TREASURES?
REVEALING PARTS OF YOURSELF THAT YOU GET TO HEAL??

LIST A TRIGGER HERE AND PULL OUT THE GOLD......ARE
THERE OTHERS? (DO THIS AS MANY TIMES AS YOU REQUIRED
TO BETTER UNDERSTAND YOURSELF.)

DOES THAT TRIGGER TIE IN WITH ANY INNER CHILD WORK
YOU DID IN EARLIER CHAPTERS? IF YOU SEE IT, EXPLAIN.

WHAT RELATIONSHIPS HAVE BEEN THE SOURCE OF YOUR BIGGEST LEARNING? LIST THE NAMES OF THOSE PEOPLE.

MINDSET: WHAT DO YOU FIND YOURSELF FOCUSING ON THE MOST THROUGHOUT YOUR DAY?

WHAT DOES ABUNDANCE FEEL LIKE TO YOU?

MAKE A LIST OF ALL THE THINGS THAT BRING YOU
JOY...SERIOUSLY...ALL THE THINGS...

MAKE A LIST OF WAYS TO PAY IT FORWARD TO SPREAD
ABUNDANCE. (REMEMBER: WHAT YOU GIVE COMES BACK)

WHAT ARE SOME DAY-TO-DAY THINGS YOU ENCOUNTER THAT
REMIND YOU OF HOW PROSPEROUS YOU ARE?

CHAPTER 11

It's Bigger Than Us

"Nothing ever goes away until it has taught us what we need to know." -Pema Chodron

Lesson 32: Soul Contracts

Soul contracts, karmic bonds, sacred contracts are written for you before your soul enters your physical body at birth. Think back to the Spiritual Ascension Guide graphic (page 93). Remember the concept of moving from 3D to 5D+?

This line of thinking falls into that awareness. We are here in these physical bodies, having these human experiences, and our ego tends to run the show. When we are in relationships, we sometimes think: How could they do this to me? Trust that it's all by design. Trust that there is a lesson for you to pull out of it for your own growth and ascension.

There are a couple different ways our souls connect with others.

Kindred spirits are close friends, like-minded people, pets, others with shared interests, beliefs, passions, tastes.

Soulmates are those we connect with an a deep level. Your best friend, your first serious relationship, your biggest fans or support people.

Twin flames (TF) are your spiritual mirrors. They activate your triggers and help your soul go through the process of awakening. Twin flame relationships are often very painful with lots of growth and transformation. They reveal the deepest feelings of pain and inadequacy. They're here to wake you up and take you higher in your ascension. These relationships are often highly passionate and very sexual. There's often an instant connection between twin flames; it is said that the soul splits in half before entering the body and the twin flame feels like home. These relationships are typically on off, on off, they come and go. They usually end when the cause of the connection is healed. It is possible to grow together and live happily ever after if both partners are willing and invested in doing their own deep healing.

Life partners provide a deep connection cultivated through love (as opposed to pain with the TF). These contracts provide a deep, sturdy, unwavering love. Lifestyles match, and deep healing takes place.

Soul contracts are all different because we are all dynamic. The purpose is to learn unconditional love. All souls are at different levels of "soul maturation." Look at your own soul contracts and karmic bonds. See the journaling prompts below. Then move on in gratitude. No more circles, cycles, negative patterns of behavior. The lesson will keep showing up until you get it!

You will be tested after acquiring your new skill. The Universe will challenge you to see if you got the lesson from the contract. More scenarios pop up to ensure you got it, to reinforce the learning, giving you the opportunity to respond in a new way. When this happens again it won't have the same power over you. You will notice the freedom and transformation in action! Soul contracts are meant to get you out of the ego, all by design.

Examples of soul contracts:

To learn forgiveness, another soul agreed to give you the experience of betrayal or mistreatment.

To learn how to be independent and strong, another soul agreed to abandon you at your worst.

To learn how to be taken care of, your soul may experience great illness.

To learn about self-esteem, assertiveness, boundaries, and empowerment, there may be another soul who has agreed to abuse you.

Get the point?

WHO KEEPS CHALLENGING YOU?

DO YOU FEEL STUCK IN SOME AREA? GET CURIOUS. WHAT IS
THE LESSON? WHAT HAVEN'T YOU LEARNED YET? FACTOR IN
YOUR CORE WOUNDING AND TRIGGERS. WHAT IS BEING
REVEALED TO YOU?

WHAT DO YOU GET TO RECEIVE FROM THE LESSON?

Lesson 33: Money Mindset

In order to advance to the next level in your life, love, and business,
you must first understand your relationship with money. We are
taking a look at the deep internal scripts that you have surrounding

Money. Completing this section of the book is just the beginning of a very exciting dynamic with a currency we all utilize in our society.

Money is simply an energetic exchange for experiences in life.

The more we raise our frequency, through focusing on positive thoughts, surrounding ourselves with positive like-minded individuals, taking care of ourselves, loving ourselves, etc., the more the Universe responds to that energy.

Money is merely a tool to get what we want. To partake in the magic of wealth consciousness, we must condition ourselves to say the "magic words": please and more, importantly: THANK YOU! In doing so, we are expressing gratitude on a fundamental level.

As we covered earlier in the book, gratitude brings in more to be grateful for, appreciation appreciates. Have an attitude of gratitude!! The more you practice gratitude, the higher your frequency vibrates, the more abundance and prosperity you allow into your life! That's the formula!!

Generally speaking, we grow up with many different scripts around Money. It is not uncommon to feel conflicted about it. Some good, most not so good.

What does all this have to do with having a history of trauma, abuse, difficult relationships? Not feeling worthy or deserving blocks the flow of money into your life!

Remember the law of attraction? Like attracts like. Abundance equals more abundance. Grateful equals more to be grateful for. Keep the focus here and you stop blocking more goodness and the flow of money into your life.

Feel grateful for all the money you do have! Pick up coins you see in the street, cash in pop bottles, clean out your wallet or purse and sage it all! Give thanks for every last penny.

Create money mantras and think them, write them, say them often!!! You have to start rewriting the scripts!! The negative, detrimental scripts around money that are really blocking more money from coming in!!

Start to look at your early programming around money.

Did you grow up not having enough? Do you feel unworthy because of that? Did your parents or primary caregivers say things like: "Money doesn't grow on trees" or "Rich people are mean or greedy or corrupt" or "We can't afford that!" Or maybe you heard the phrase: "Filthy rich," which definitely has a dirty connotation.

How do you feel about paying bills?? Are you annoyed or frustrated at all them?? Have you thought about what you're getting in exchange for the bill??

Be thankful when paying bills!

Express gratitude for each service the bill provides. Adopt this mentality with debt, too (if applicable).

Living in debt is temporary.

Borrowing that money or charging on your credit card has allowed you to have something before having the cash. Knowing that you're repaying it and clearing that energy is a positive way to view the debt.

Have you ever tracked all the money you have coming in? Deliberately writing it all down?

Have you ever called in a specific amount of money by a specific day?? That is entirely possible! Give that money a place to go and be open to receiving it!!

Take inspired action when called to do so and trust that it's all on its way.

I have manifested a lot of money this way!!

It's true and it's happened because I declared it all ahead of time, let go of the HOW and trusted the process!!

Or what about your habits and mindsct around tipping those in the service industry?? I love to tip extremely generously because I appreciate their hard work (if it's warranted) and I KNOW the money I pay out returns to me tenfold!! I know that to be true because I declare it!! I give thanks, genuinely feel grateful as I'm tipping and I trust that the money is coming back in abundance!

The reality is that money is an amplifier!

And it's just paper, we are the ones who give it power.

Money offers an energetic exchange. When we pay for things we're getting something in return! It's just a currency. Like our time, our attention, the love we give.

When we invest in ourselves it's a reflection of our own self-worth! Going to school, taking classes, hiring a coach of any kind (fitness, business, life) those are all investments in ourselves.

And those are so necessary because we're able to fast track the results we are aiming for by working with someone much more experienced with the process!! How grateful are you of people like that!!

Now, if there's a feeling of lack around money or scarcity, feeling worried, stressed, doubtful, jealous, discouraged these feelings are not going to bring you more money ever. Complaining, arguing, getting frustrated, etc., will only make the situation worse.

Unfortunately, coming from a history of trauma or abuse, these emotions tend to be a mindset, yours or your parents that has been passed down to you so it's up to YOU to turn this ship around!! It takes practice and conscious choices around language and feelings about money. It can be done!!

They're just thoughts and thoughts can be changed!

IN THIS MOMENT: ARE YOUR BASIC NEEDS MET? DO YOU HAVE FOOD? SHELTER? EDUCATION? BOOKS YOU CAN READ? A VEHICLE? A JOB? ETC. ALL THESE COST MONEY SO EXPRESS GRATITUDE FOR THEM. REMEMBER: COMPLAINING WILL STOP THE FLOW OF MONEY ENERGETICALLY AND THE UNIVERSE SEES, HEARS, FEELS THIS!!

LIST 3-5 THINGS YOU REMEMBER YOUR PARENTS OR OTHER CAREGIVERS SAYING ABOUT MONEY. FOR JUST THIS ONCE FOCUS ON THE NEGATIVE, PESSIMISTIC PHRASES YOU'VE HEARD ABOUT THIS TOPIC.

TAKE AT LEAST ONE OF THESE PHRASES AND BREAK IT DOWN.
IS IT TRUE? IS IT POSSIBLE TO DISPROVE THIS DEEPLY
INGRAINED NEGATIVE BELIEF ABOUT MONEY?

CREATE A POSITIVE VERSION OF THIS SCRIPT, A MANTRA OR
AFFIRMATION, THAT YOU CAN WRITE ON POST-ITS OR IN YOUR
JOURNAL REPEATEDLY, SET AN ALARM ON YOUR PHONE JUST
TO BE REMINDED OF YOUR NEW PROGRAMMING OFTEN!

LIST 3-5 POSITIVE PHRASES ABOUT MONEY. TAKING THAT A STEP FURTHER, FILL THIS LIST WITH ALL THE POSITIVE EXPERIENCES MONEY ALLOWS YOU TO HAVE.

WRITE MONEY A LOVE NOTE. THINK OF THIS AS A RELATIONSHIP YOU ARE IN WITH ANOTHER INDIVIDUAL. THAT IS THE ENERGY WE SEND OUT AND RECEIVE FROM THE UNIVERSE. DO YOU LOVE MONEY AND ARE EXCITED BY THE PROSPECTS? DO YOU APPRECIATE THE RELIEF AND STABILITY THAT COMES FROM HAVING MORE OF IT? DOES IT SCARE YOU? DO YOU FEEL YOU CAN TRUST IT? ARE YOU (SUBCONSCIOUSLY) PUSHING MONEY AWAY OUT OF A DESIRE TO PROTECT YOURSELF FROM ITS ABANDONMENT? DO YOU WANT TO GROW AND SUCCEED TOGETHER? ENJOY ENRICHING, FUN EXPERIENCES TOGETHER? WRITE ON A SEPARATE SHEET IF NECESSARY.

CREATE SOME MONEY MANTRAS FOR YOURSELF. HERE ARE A FEW TO CHOOSE FROM:

I LOVE MONEY BECAUSE IT GIVES ME FREEDOM AND OPTIONS.

I LOVE MONEY AND MONEY LOVES ME!
I AM A MAGNET FOR MONEY!

PROSPERITY IS DRAWN TO ME!

MONEY COMES TO ME EASILY AND ALL THE TIME!
I LOVE MONEY BECAUSE IT ALLOWS ME TO BE MORE OF WHO I AM.

LIST 10 REASONS WHY YOU ARE GRATEFUL FOR MONEY

1. _____

2. _____

3. _____

4. _____

5. _____

6. _____

7. _____

8. _____

9. _____

10. _____

CHAPTER 12

On Divine Assignment

"Passion is that feeling that tells you: this is the right thing to do. Nothing can stand in my way. It doesn't matter what anyone else says. This feeling is so good that it cannot be ignored. I'm going to follow my bliss and act upon this glorious sensation of joy."

-Wayne Dyer

Lesson 34: Passions

Have you ever looked at the word "Inspired" and thought of "in-spirit"??

When we feel enthusiastic about something, when something brings us joy, lights a fire within us, when you feel energized talking about something thats how we know it's part of our Divine Assignment.

In Part I, I went into great detail about my own Divine Assignments.

We are all given our own **natural abilities** that are channeled through The Universe/Source/God. In doing what you love, what you are good at, you're making a positive impact on the world because your love and authenticity for "it" can be felt!!

Remember the vibrations!!?! Think of what brings you into the high vibe states.

The good vibes bring on optimal health, happiness, optimism. From this place we are able to heal and open the heart... moving towards more positive mental shifts!

When we're in the higher vibrational states we can see new opportunities, we are energized by our visions, we are receptive to the energy flowing through us, we feel guided, supported and nourished by this flow of positive energy!!

In sharing our unique gifts, we light the way, lifting each other up to our highest potential and our FULLEST expression!!

Return home to SELF! Remember who you are.

SOOOOO.... WHAT LIGHTS YOU UP? WHAT EXCITES YOU? WHAT MAKES YOU FEEL GREAT ENTHUSIASM? WHAT STIRS YOUR SOUL?

WHAT IS SOMETHING YOU COULD TALK FOR HOURS AND HOURS ABOUT? IF MONEY WASN'T A CONCERN, WHAT WOULD YOU BE DOING IN LIFE?

WHAT IS YOUR "WHY"? WHAT MOTIVATES YOU TO KEEP
SHOWING UP?

WHAT ARE YOUR STRENGTHS? LIST 10-20+ OF THEM.

IN THE YOGIC PHILOSOPHY OF HINDUISM, THIS IS REFERRED
TO AS YOUR "DHARMA"...YOUR RIGHT WAY TO LIVE, MOST
ALIGNED WITH YOUR SOUL'S PURPOSE. DESCRIBE WHAT THIS
MIGHT BE FOR YOU.

DO YOU HAVE ANY BLOCKS OR BARRIERS AROUND THIS CONCEPT? ARE YOU OPEN TO RECEIVE?

WHAT ACTIVITIES MAKE YOU LOSE TRACK OF TIME?

THINK TO YOURSELF: WHAT IS YOUR INVOLVEMENT WITH SOCIAL MEDIA? INSTAGRAM, FACEBOOK, TWITTER, ETC. WHAT SORT OF CONTENT DOES YOUR FEED CONSIST OF? UPLIFTING AND POSITIVE OR DRAINING AND NEGATIVE?

Lesson 35: The Law of Attraction (LOA)

This stuff really gets me pumped up!!!! Don't get me wrong....I love all the nerdy psychological and physiological stuff too...and this is also all right up my alley!!

The **Law of Attraction (LOA)** is a law of the Universe! There are twelve Spiritual Laws of the Universe. Based on quantum physics, using the Power of the Mind to attract the reality we want to be living.

Read: THOUGHTS BECOME THINGS!!! Thoughts and EMOTIONS have their own frequencies. I think I have drilled that home by now!

What we are feeling, we are emitting out to the Universe and in turn, people/situations/dynamics are echoed back to you that align with those frequencies. You are constantly creating your world, whether you know it or not. Focus on the good, get more good. Focus on worrying or "the bad," get more things to worry about or "the bad" brought back to you.

If you are caught up in shitty emotions like fear and anger, you are going to attract more experiences/people that cause more fear and anger to arise. #facts

On the other hand, if you are resonating LOVE, JOY, ABUNDANCE, PROSPERITY you will undoubtably attract more of that awesome-ness!!

The energy you put out to the Universe comes back to you!

This is essential to your understanding of manifesting.

We have to align with the same frequency of all we are drawing in through the LOA.

It's all about the feels, remember?

The Universal Law of Attraction

ASK

Ask for what you truly want. Be clear, specific AF and really feeeeel it.

BELIEVE

Believe you already have it. See yourself living your life with all the abundance and magic you are calling in. FEEL yourself in this life. Align your frequency to that of your wishes.

RECEIVE

Be grateful and give thanks for all that is on its way. Trust and surrender to the process. Allow yourself to receive on all levels energetically to keep the flow open.

The psycho-physiological (mind-body) connection comes into play in a profound way. This is when thoughts influence the physiological reactions of the body. And as we know, our physiology also leads the way the majority of the time.

Special attention needs to be paid to the concept of conscious languaging (terminology, expressions, semantics, wording).

We are all energetic beings. The words we speak (and those we think) have a profound effect on us. It is common to choose negative feelings, thought and phrases. All the I can'ts, I don't, I should, I shouldn't, I won't, etc are extremely detrimental to the person expressing themselves in this manner. You are matching your energy field up with that which you don't want. When these words are thought or spoken, you are turning over your personal power. Hidden in the can'ts and won'ts are your desires. It is necessary to flip the wording into its positive expression.

Everything has a frequency, a vibration, an energy. Whatever you feel on this vibration brings more of this vibration into your life. Water carries this energy. We are approximately 70% water.

Thoughts are energy, and energy properly channeled has the power to transform you, your life, and your entire universe! LIKE ATTRACTS LIKE.

....what you give out, you receive back!!

There is power in the vibration of each word. Purposefully moving away from classic birthing associations, these redefined terms will help support you on your healing journey.

In order to advance to the next level in life and in business, we must forgive to make space for the new!!

If we are holding onto the low vibe feelings/shitty energy (e.g.: negative feelings, hurt, trauma, betrayals, etc) then we are STUCK and no matter how much you want to move forward, it won't happen.

When we forgive and genuinely release "it," we remove the resentment and are free to ascend towards our highest self, ready to receive all we are actively calling in with our New Moon Intentions and any other manifestation practices you may have.

When we do this deep healing, clear the blocks we have around not feeling worthy or "good enough," are open to receive, we set ourselves up to welcome in the ABUNDANCE that is naturally all around us, within us, waiting for us to give it all permission to come in.

Lesson 36: Manifestation

This is based on living by the LOA!! Consciously co-creating the world you live in, experiencing a life beyond your WiLdeSt dreams! You must trust in a higher power.

When manifesting, it is important to:

- Focus on gratitude and all you appreciate!! This helps raise your vibration and keeps you higher with your frequency. Stay positive!

- Speak it, Think it, Feel it like its already done: Align your frequency with that you're calling in

- Avoid thinking about what you don't want: Remember... flip it positively!

- Visualize, meditate, journal on that which you are calling in

- Trust and surrender that what you are calling in is on its way to you

I work with manifesting every day. I liken manifestation to putting an order in online and trusting that the order will be delivered. When I was driving a lot in my pediatric nursing job, I noticed delivery trucks often. To me, they represented my manifestations coming true.

There was a short period of time when I was seeing them yet they were driving away from me, which meant my dreams were taking a detour! I said to the Universe: "start showing the delivery trucks driving towards me" as confirmation that my manifestations were on their way. Sure enough, they all started driving in my direction!! I believe in signs like that. It was supportive and affirming that my desires were coming. We have to trust it!!

Take a look at your thoughts and emotions on a regular basis. Are they positive and uplifting or negative and critical?

Allow yourself to get into a practice of thinking positive thoughts.

CREATE SOME POSITIVE AFFIRMATIONS THAT WORK TO SUPPORT YOU IN CALLING IN WHAT YOU DESIRE, UNIQUE TO YOUR LIFE AND PERSONAL SITUATION. BE SURE TO PHRASE THEM IN THE PRESENT TENSE, KEEP THEM POSITIVE ("SMILE" VS "DON'T FROWN"), BE SPECIFIC.

CREATE SOME "I AM" STATEMENTS ABOUT YOURSELF NOW
AND EVERY SINGLE DAY. POSITIVE, UPLIFTING, HAPPY,
CONSTRUCTIVE STATEMENTS ABOUT YOURSELF!

Pay attention to the New Moon's every month. I remind my community to write out your New Moon Intentions. See free downloads on my site (www.karakaraoguz.com) for 5 Tips to Step Up Your Manifestation Game!!

Lesson 37: Your Big Picture Vision

This is your life!

You've just sorted through some really serious shit in this book! You've cleared a ton of maladaptive responses, dysfunctional tendencies and patterns. Remember, those are not who you are, they are merely part of who you were...before you learned that they were your body's beautiful ability to protect and adapt!

So now you're about to get really specific and crystal clear on what you want your life to look and feel like!!

It is my hope that, at this point, you have a very clear understanding of who you are and how you feel about love, and have a solid foundation of incorporating mindfulness into your life. I hope you have better insights into how you feel about your sense of belonging, being a part of community, your soul tribe, understanding your family of origin, attachments in love, your nervous system, dynamics with your significant other, your core wounding, shadow work, inner child work, reparenting, boundaries, forgiveness, intimacy, how effing important it is to repair, and what is needed to draw in more of what you want and manifest a life beyond your WiLdeSt dreams!!

As we have heard many times throughout our time together, *energy is everything*. Your visualizations are very powerful. And of course, how you feel about something matters a lot.

WHAT IS YOUR BIG PICTURE VISION FOR YOURSELF? LET YOURSELF DREAM BIG! THINK OF YOUR LIFESTYLE TOO...

WRITE OUT YOUR IDEAL DAY FROM THE MOMENT YOU CRACK YOUR EYES OPEN TO THE MOMENT YOU LAY YOUR HEAD DOWN ON YOUR PILLOW AT NIGHT.

HOW DO YOU WANT TO FEEL?

What, if any, stories do you have around being **SEEN**? Taking up space? Shining bright in all your awesomeness, living as authentically as possible? Is it safe? Would it make someone feel bad? Are you afraid of judgment? Ridicule?

At this point in your life, what is standing in your way to receive all the beauty, joy, peace, abundance that is meant for you?

ARE YOU READY TO BE LIVING THE LIFE OF YOUR DREAMS??

WHAT ARE **AT LEAST** THREE ACTIONABLE STEPS YOU CAN TAKE TO ENSURE THAT YOU ARE LIVING WITH INTENTION?

1.

2.

3.

WRITE OUT YOUR IDEAL RELATIONSHIP, BE AS SPECIFIC AS
POSSIBLE, WHETHER YOU ARE SINGLE NOW AND ARE CALLING
IN WHAT YOUR FUTURE PARTNER LOOKS LIKE OR IF YOU ARE
COUPLED AND ARE WANTING THE DYNAMIC TO BE DIFFERENT.
REMEMBER, "WHEN YOU CHANGE THE WAY YOU LOOK AT
THINGS, THE THINGS YOU LOOK AT CHANGE."-WAYNE DYER

If you are coupled, think about how, when we start showing up
differently, the people we engage with start to shift too.

Once you have written out your ideal day and your ideal relationship,
revisit them often. Embody the emotions, feeeeel what it is like to
have that be true. Celebrate any forward momentum getting you
closer towards your ideal life!!

Lesson 38: Living With Intention

In order to Live With Intention, you first have to know who you are and where you are heading. Living with Intention consists of:

- Being aware of your dreams
- Setting goals
- Making conscious choices
- Co-creating a life beyond your WiLdeSt dreams!

TAKING INSPIRED ACTION that is aligned with how you want to feel in this life!!

INTENTION is the energy behind it allllllllllll!

Without intention, presence is hollow and unstable... empty, really... ((ugh, sounds awful!)). It's THAT simple, My Love.

KEEP SHOWING UP

PART III: THE WRAP UP

CHAPTER 13

Bringing It All Together

"Peace. It does not mean to be in a place of no noise, trouble or hard work. It means to be in the midst of those things and still be calm in your heart." -Unknown

For years, I felt a strong pull to write this book. I trust that all works out in divine order and this book has landed in your hands at the perfect time in your life. A time when you are ready for change and ready, willing, and able to receive these lessons.

In my own healing journey, there were a couple major players when it came to breaking the dysfunctional patterns I had been used to. All were covered in Part II. The revelations and learning that were most influential were radical self love, the Polyvagal Theory, attachment styles, the five stages of grief, healthy boundaries, and remembering we are a soul in this physical body (sacred contracts).

Pobody is Nerfect. I am not exempt from dysfunctional, codependent tendencies. Though my commitment to healing and showing up is strong and ever present, I strive to be a better person every single day.

The residual effects of my earlier traumas have left me caring a little too much about how my plates are stacked or how my towels are folded. I have a need to be in the driver's seat (literally!) whenever I go on adventures with friends (they all know and accept me). My king-sized bed has to be a certain way with my pillows and comforter in place before I can fully relax and drift off to dreamland. It is not uncommon to need to exert control over your surroundings when you've been in situations as a child where you didn't have control.

It is so important to understand your own trauma (as well as your partners', if coupled). Having an awareness of your own barriers to love will serve you very well.

This can be a complicated thing, though my hope is: since you've taken in all the lessons in this book, you now have a tremendous understanding of who you are. And more importantly: WHY you are the way you are.

You've put your own puzzle pieces together. You've connected all the dots. Becoming aware of your own dynamics within conflict, attachment styles, and what your nervous system does in response to threats that come up in relationships with others is so so so important to help you positively navigate conflict. Hold yourself in a soft, compassionate space as you heal. You are unlearning and relearning. Be good to you.

It took quite a while to understand all this for myself though once it all clicked I began feeling so much relief. Like I wasn't crazy!

Know that there is hella overlap here. Those with porous boundaries often have anxious attachments and typically fawn when it comes to conflict. This was me. I wanted to connect to others and be close. If there was conflict, I would state my position then later back down, and do all I could to smooth things over so I wouldn't feel so distant and awful, though there hadn't been any real repair or resolution. On the other end of the spectrum, those with rigid boundaries often have avoidant attachments and tend to shutdown, unpacking in the dorsal vagal state of the nervous system.

We each need to do our own work around the **core wounds**. These present a major barrier to love. Thinking we're not "good enough" or deserving of someone else's love. It's not up to you to decide how much someone else loves you!! Sometimes people don't know where to begin with their healing and don't even know what they can do to help themselves. In addition to reading this book, continue educating yourself. And, if coupled, it is most beneficial when both parties are willing to do the work.

Remember that we attract others who are sacred mirrors to our internal story line. How we're able to show up for others is very revealing about our own inner landscape. People typically treat others the way they feel about themselves. How you choose to love or not love, show affection or not, communicate effectively or not all show us where we are in our process of growth and ascension. We see where our work remains, in those areas that seem to fall short.

We can spend years doing the deeply healing inner work on ourselves alone then get into a partnership and see a whole other slew of issues unfold. I experienced this after my divorce and before the TF. I thought I was so grounded by myself, ready to live happily ever after then human, ego shit came on the scene and attachment wounds reared their ugly head. I didn't recognize myself. It was no fun at all. Here's the fact of the matter: We get hurt in relationships and we heal in relationships. Period. Align with others who support your growth, believe in helping you navigate the healing you're working on, and cheer you on as you hit new levels of awareness.

There is a constant interplay with the world around us, calling on us to connect to self or disconnect from self. Barriers or blocks to intimacy happen when we get caught up in the Shadow self, that part of yourself you want to reject. Remember, when the Shadow self is in the behind the wheel, we tend to disconnect which blocks intimacy with your loved one. Go back and revisit your core wounds. You may withhold intimacy or love, be reactive, judgmental, critical, have fears or insecurities come up, you may look for retribution, be contemptuous, you may lash out. Maybe you have avoidant tactics where you shut down, ignore, are incapable of formulating any sort of response to your significant other. Maybe you have an anxious style of attachment and you may get really freaking needy and have a deep desire for closeness, even within all the chaos of the Shadow self coming up for one or both of you. Whatever the case may be, remember that we are always trying to move ourselves towards perceived safety!!

I love you and I am so proud of you for showing up and doing this work!!!

Ways to work with me:

- 1:1 private client (limited availability), 3- and 6- month packages
- Group programs offered throughout the year
  - Soul Ascension Academy, a 6-week Online Group Coaching
  - Wounded to Worthy, a 4-week Online Group Coaching
- Various workshops and classes also offered throughout the year
  - Empowered Empath Masterclass
  - Soul Ascension 3-Day Activation
  - Know Your Worth Workshop
- Online learning courses are available for immediate download on my website **www.karakaraoguz.com**
  - Gratitude For Daysss 5-day series
  - Connecting To Your Intuition 3 day series
  - Polyvagal Theory and Your ANS
  - Heart and Soul, a 21-Day self-study course

ACKNOWLEDGMENTS

I'd like to thank my ex-husband, baby daddy Alex for all his support and encouragement. We met as teens, spent 12 years together as a couple (married for seven years) and now co-parent like bosses together for our amazing young men. It's a good thing I didn't have him killed after our divorce when I really wanted to hire a hitman! Alex, you've shown me that people do change and they can come around and be really freaking good people even if there was a time when priorities were a little screwy. Thanks for being one of my biggest fans, always cheering me on, celebrating my wins, and helping me turn my L's into lessons! And thanks for being a good dad and role model to the young men, breaking generational trauma in your own right so our boys can have a different experience than you had.

My guys, AB and LB, you both have made me a better person. In showing up being your mom, I have had to heal my own stuff so I don't pass it on to you. You show me unconditional love. You know the sky is the limit! Always be yourself, trust your intuition, know your worth, and trust that money is everywhere! You are deserving of it all!! If you can believe it, you can achieve it. Make it happen!

Thanks to my good GF's (TW, ML, AK, JS, MM) for checking in on me during my intense grieving process when I didn't want to have contact with anyone. Your love and support helped carry me.

Thank you to my volunteer book editors (JR, JS, TW, KS, ER) who gave me valuable feedback and tremendous support and encouragement as I brought it all together.

Thanks to my cousin Emilie for always being there for me, day or night. And for helping tremendously with final, final, FINAL book edits ;) I am so pumped for our future travel adventures! I love you!!

Thanks to Karen, my Gyps. I am so grateful to walk this path side by side with you. You reflect back to me all the important things in life. You mean so much to me.

Thank you to my clients who allow me into such a sacred space, your deep healing. You trust me to support you through some serious reflections and I am so honored to walk the path with you.

Thanks to my Rising Sisterhood Mastermind ladies for continuing to inspire me and lift me higher. I so value your ambition and strength. We're here to make a difference and have an amazing lasting impact on the world!

Resources

The Way of The Superior Man David Deida

Homecoming: Reclaiming and Championing Your Inner Child John Bradshaw

The Polyvagal Theory in Therapy Deb Dana

The Body Keeps the Score Bessel van Der Kolk, MD

Waking the Tiger Peter Levine

Attached Dr Amir Levine and Rachel SF Heller, MA

Keeping the LOVE You Find Harville Hendrix PhD and Helen LaKelly Hunt PhD

You are a Badass Jen Sincero

You are a Badass at Making Money Jen Sincero

Get Rich Lucky Bitch Denise Duffield-Thomas

Ask and It Is Given Esther and Jerry Hicks

Becoming Supernatural Dr. Joe Dispenza

Spirit Junkie Gabrielle Bernstein

The Universe Has Your Back Gabby Bernstein

Super Attractor Gabrielle Bernstein

Steering by Starlight Martha Beck

Finding Your Way in a Wild New World Martha Beck

The Four Agreements Don Miguel Ruiz

Daring Greatly Brene Brown

The Power of Now Eckhart Tolle

A New Earth Eckhart Tolle

Can't Hurt Me David Goggins

Big Magic Elizabeth Gilbert

Light is the New Black Rebecca Campbell

Daily Love Mastin Kipp

The Untethered Soul Michael Singer

The Surrender Experiment Michael Singer

The Big Leap Gay Hendricks

You Can Heal Your Life Louise Hay

The Power is Within You Louise Hay

KEEP SHOWING UP

Made in the USA
Middletown, DE
28 September 2020

20742402R00146